"I like *The End of Worry* for two reasons: first, it will help life's worriers to worry less; and second, I know that vulnerable people are in safe hands with the authors. This book strikes a rare balance in its presentation of liberating truth. It is both scientifically informed and theologically sound; it is both realistic and at the same time faith promoting. *The End of Worry* is in effect a practical commentary on the greatest advice ever given on worry—Jesus' statement: 'Do not worry about tomorrow, for tomorrow will worry about itself. Each day has enough trouble of its own.' (Matthew 6:34)"

—Peter Anderson, lead pastor of Destiny Church, Edinburgh

"Based on cognitive-behavior therapy principles and a scientific understanding of worry, the psychology throughout the book is sound. For those who seek guidance and inspiration in the Bible, the authors offer a thoughtful way of approaching verses that may be confusing for those who are prone to worry. The balance between reflection and action is nicely struck, and with worksheets that link the two together, people can plan what to do and how to go about doing it. Finally, the book is written from a very personal perspective, showing real insight into the world of the worrier, and, most importantly, it is written with compassion."

—Professor Mark Freeston,
professor of clinical psychology at Newcastle University, UK

"Jesus didn't say, 'There's nothing to worry about,' but 'Don't worry in spite of everything there is to worry about.' Will van der Hart and Rob Waller tackle this key issue in many people's lives."

—Nicky Gumbel, vicar of Holy Trinity Brompton, London

"One of the hardest verses in the Bible is 'Do not worry,' and I was therefore intrigued by *The End of Worry*. Well, I couldn't put it down! It is honest, humorous, and holistic. I was re-educated and I am already seeing the benefits."

—Canon J. John, author and evangelist

"A very thoughtful, balanced, and practical approach to the reality of anxiety. The authors have authority to write on worry, not only because they know the subject very well, but especially because they have a passion to help others with the same spirit as the Great Physician: reaching the whole person and not only their emotions. *The End of Worry* goes far beyond the practical help of a mere self-help book; it is a therapeutic tool that is solidly founded on the Scriptures."

—Dr. Pablo Martinez, author and psychiatrist

"This easy-to-read mix of pastoral counsel, biblical exposition, personal experience, plentiful anecdotes, and practical exercises will help many anxious Christians to recognize and break free from the 'worry rules' that prevent them from enjoying the perfect love that overcomes all fear."

—Dr. Trevor Stammers, former general practitioner
and chair of Christian Medical Fellowship 2007–2010

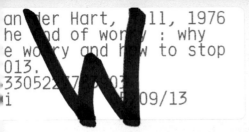
THE END OF
WORRY

WHY WE WORRY AND HOW TO STOP

☹ 😐 ☺ ☹ 😐 ☺ ☹ 😐 ☺ ☹ 😐 ☺ ☹ 😐 ☺

WILL VAN DER HART
AND ROB WALLER

Howard Books
A Division of Simon & Schuster, Inc.
New York   Nashville   London   Toronto   Sydney   New Delhi

To those who worry

Howard Books
A Division of Simon & Schuster, Inc.
1230 Avenue of the Americas
New York, NY 10020

Copyright © 2011 by Will van der Hart and Rob Waller

This work was originally published in Great Britain in 2011
by Inter-Varsity Press as *The Worry Book*.

Scripture quotations are taken from the Holy Bible, New International Version.

Copyright © 1973, 1978, 1984 by International Bible Society. Used by permission of
Hodder & Stoughton, a division of Hodder Headline Ltd. All rights reserved. NW is a
trademark of International Bible Society. UK trademark number 1448790.

Scripture quotations marked *ESV* are from The Holy Bible, English Standard
Version, published by HarperCollins Publishers © 2001 by Crossway Bibles,
a division of Good News Publishers. Used by permission. All rights reserved.

First Howard Books trade paperback edition February 2013

HOWARD and colophon are trademarks of Simon & Schuster, Inc.

For information about special discounts for bulk purchases,
please contact Simon & Schuster Special Sales at 1-866-506-1949
or business@simonandschuster.com.

The Simon & Schuster Speakers Bureau can bring authors to your live event.
For more information or to book an event contact the Simon & Schuster Speakers
Bureau at 1-866-248-3049 or visit our website at www.simonspeakers.com.

Designed by Davina Mock-Maniscalco

Manufactured in the United States of America

1   3   5   7   9   10   8   6   4   2

Library of Congress Cataloging-in-Publication Data
Van der Hart, Will, 1976–
The end of worry : why we worry and how to stop /
Will van der Hart and Rob Waller.
p. cm.
Includes bibliographical references.
1. Worry. 2. Peace of mind. I. Waller, Rob. II. Title.
BF575.W8V36 2013
152.4'6—dc23   2012022051

ISBN 978-1-4516-8280-9
ISBN 978-1-4516-8281-6 (ebook)

Contents

Acknowledgments

Rob would like to thank his employers at NHS Lothian for their continued support throughout his employment, as well as during his training, and Will thanks his colleagues and friends in the diocese of London, particularly Bishops Richard and Pete.

We are grateful to the editorial and marketing team at IVP (Eleanor, Marie, Kath, and Daryl) for their skill and patience in working with our many drafts, but also for sharing our vision for this book.

We are both indebted to our wives, Susanna and Lucinda, and to our families far more than we can say; and of course to our God, who has taught us much about worry, love, and the hope we share.

Foreword

This book shows that we all worry. There are times when it overwhelms us and gets out of control, but here we are shown what we can do to ease our tendency to worry.

The text is open, honest, and talks about real life. Rob and Will do not just rely on the case studies of others, but speak of their own personal problems, demonstrating that even ministers and psychiatrists can be affected by disease and worry. One tip that especially stuck in my mind was remembering to view the big picture. The book contains a good analogy about traffic jams and how we need perspective and an overview, rather than just thinking about the car in front while we are going nowhere.

For those suffering with mental-health issues in addition to worry, this book affirms that these are valid, despite what some folks from the "pull-your-socks-up" school would say.

There are many reasons to commend *The End of Worry*. It is scripturally supported and advocates aspects of prayer, care, and community. It uses a cognitive-behavioral approach, which can be very successful. It not only tells how to deal with the problem, but explains the why of worry: what's going on in the background. It also provides evidence that worry has a physiological impact. In addition, it shows that worry is not something we simply have to put up with. No, it gives the reader steps to follow in order to "recover" from being a chronic worrier. The exercises and reflective work at the end of the chapters are very useful in leading the reader on a progressive journey.

Counselors and pastors will benefit enormously from not only reading this book but also by having it on their bookshelves to recommend to clients and parishioners.

—Greta Randle,
chief executive of the Association of Christian Counselors,
May 2011

Preface

Many of us are consumed by worry, yet we fail to talk about the "invisible" problem. As a church leader and someone who has battled worry all his life, Will knows the persistence of the problem, the simplicity of the answer, and yet the length of the journey. As a psychiatrist, Rob offers some of the theory, but blends it with a biblically informed perspective of hope and healing.

We have not written a triumphalist response to the problem. In many ways, it would feel far more comfortable to write of simple obedience to the scriptures about "not worrying," and to tell people to "pray harder." Yet we know from personal and professional experience that even the most determined and convicted Christian can remain ensnared by worry. Many great past and current Christian leaders—John Bunyan, Martin Luther, and Charles Spurgeon, to name but a few—have quietly admitted that their freedom and joy have been fettered by anxiety. We suspect that their reluctance to share these battles more publicly stems from a fear that to do so would weaken their witness and their leadership. And perhaps our own struggle with writing about these issues demonstrates a similar fear in us.

But the fear to address the experience of worry has led to a culture of shame and silence regarding the issue. In Will's work with the church, and in Rob's work with the National Health Service (NHS), and in our speaking nationally on issues of emotional health, a universal cross-section of people confess to being consumed by worry, while also being deeply ashamed about their inability to exhibit a simple trust in God. In only a very few instances have people expressed any awareness of the contribution of psychological factors. Christians tend to believe that the problem is purely spiritual—one of simple disobedience and lack of trust. It is no surprise then that they often feel too ashamed either to acknowledge that a problem exists or to seek help to overcome it.

Within this book you will find what we hope is a balanced look at the issue of persistent and problematic worry. It is our hope that what you read will be compassionate and humane, not a study of complex theology or science. We are, after all, fellow travelers through the rough landscape of worry and perfectionism, and much of what we are sharing comes out of the hard-won lessons of our own battles for freedom and joy in God's faithfulness to us.

Introduction

I've developed a new philosophy!
I only dread one day at a time. . . .
CHARLIE BROWN (CHARLES M. SCHULZ)

People who worry are preoccupied with tomorrow—what might happen and what could go wrong. However, there is also the deeper awareness that tomorrow is not being changed by this worry, and that instead today is filled only with head-aches. This perspective is different from that of the person who is anxious about a specific fear, such as public speaking or of the person who is depressed and more focused on the past.

If you are reading this book, it is likely that you or someone you know has a significant problem with worry. Of course, we all worry from time to time, but you may be unable to turn it off and escape. Worry has become something that takes up a large part of the day, and possibly the night, too. Life seems to have become uncontrollable, with lots of worries about problems to which you don't have an answer. You carry tension in your body, and this is beginning to have an effect on your self-esteem, your relationships, and even your physical health.

What Is Worry?

Will is a worrier. He always has been, and at times this is obvious . Worry became a real problem after the London bombings in 2005 when his church was used as a base for the emergency services (you'll read more of this story in Chapter 2, "Understanding My Worry"). He sought counseling in the form of cognitive-behavioral therapy and has also received treatment from his general practitioner. It is an ongoing battle, and he still tends to worry when things pile up—understandable, but usually out of proportion to the issues at hand. He is writing this book because he has had to live by its principles every day. Good friends, good habits, and a raw, authentic faith are vital to his staying on track.

Rob is not a typical worrier; in fact, most people think he is laid back. But actually he is a perfectionist who uses attempts at perfection to control and keep his worries at bay. The laid-back bit is an act. This means he can aim for perfection in areas where it really doesn't matter—you should have seen the first drafts of this book, which were immaculately formatted! He struggles with letting go and dislikes it when he is not directing things, and he can actually feel quite uncomfortable when others take charge. However, he is also immensely grateful to his wife, who loves him regardless and refuses to plan every detail of every weekend—and over the years he has even learned how to relax and enjoy the moment. God has also "refused to conform" to the patterns set and has taken him to places that are far more fun—though the journey has been "worrying" at times.

Worry is an individual experience and it differs among people, but there are patterns that can help us isolate the specific categories. Doctors call severe worry generalized anxiety disorder (GAD). This is characterized by worries about things that feel uncontrollable, accompanied by restlessness, a proneness to fatigue, difficulty in concentrating, irritability, muscle tension, and disturbed sleep. The national guidelines on GAD report that 44 in every 1,000 adults will experience this severe worry. [1] GAD is also a feature of other mental-health problems, including some forms of depression in which a person can worry about the future as well as the past (88 per 1,000 people). Less severe forms of worry are even more common (164 per 1,000 people).

Worry has a significant impact on how people live. Worried individuals may be unable to work for periods of time or may work with reduced productivity. They may see the doctor a number of times without getting help, although most people who worry have done so for many years before even starting to seek assistance. They may worry that they have an underlying physical illness which they cannot be reassured about, resulting in lots of medical tests and the additional anxieties these produce.

Worry is not something that is immediately obvious to those around you. And it tends to be something in the background of our minds, like a haze or buzz that is always there. From time to time, there will also be more extreme worries that punctuate the haze, but these will rarely result in outright panic. Panic attacks can and do happen (and we have included some information on these at the end of the book), but for most people, worry will be more chronic, characterized by "getting by" or "struggling on through." Others may notice panic attacks and offer sympathy, but this sympathy ends when the problem seems to stop. Except it hasn't stopped—it has just gone underground.

In the case of worry, the anxiety rarely peaks into panic but also rarely disappears completely. It's a bit like being in a dentist's waiting room while other people's names are being called out. The spikes of adrenalin each time the speaker (receptionist) comes to life are not as bad as the tension of waiting in between.

How Can I Get Help?

Getting help for worry can be difficult. This is partly because, as mentioned above, others may not think someone has a problem, as the worrier will tend to keep overt anxiety at bay most of the time. Family members, coworkers, and fellow parishioners may not grasp that someone really is struggling inside. This makes worry different from problems such as depression and from specific worries, such as a fear of social situations or heights, which have a more noticeable effect on one's emotions and behavior.

Depression and specific fears are also better understood. There are a number of good books on these, and a general practitioner should be confident about when to start medication or refer a patient for therapy. But worriers can often be dismissed as not really ill, just needing to rest for a bit (which is not helpful, by the way), and others can think they are wasting time. There is also a lack of information on the subject, as research on worry has lagged behind other mental-health problems.

All of these problems can be compounded in the Christian world, where informed books are even scarcer, advice is forthcoming but often unhelpful, and expectations are exceptionally high. Worriers feel they are disobeying God, lacking in faith, and misunderstood by those in their church.

This book is an attempt to set that record straight and offer help, drawing on the latest advances in therapy and on the authors' insights into the unique problems that worrying Christians face. It is a comprehensive overview of the problems, the obstacles and the landscape of worry, ultimately offering a way out. Each chapter covers a core topic, such as the nature of worry, why we all have favorite "worry themes," and how our faith is involved (for better and for worse). It will also take you on a journey from your individual worries to an understanding of the process of worry, from trying to make an uncertain world certain to developing a tolerance of uncertainty. We will map out a way to change, learn a new way to view your thoughts, and end up feeling better as a result.

The Charlie Brown quote at the beginning of this chapter is there for a reason: Charlie Brown has made a start on dealing with his worry—he's doing it one day at a time! This might not sound like a big step, but if your worry seems uncontrollable and tends to extend to everything and for all future times, you will realize what a milestone this is. Jesus says something similar in Matthew 6:34: "Do not worry about tomorrow, for tomorrow will worry about itself. Each day has enough trouble of its own." It's now time to start the journey out of worry, and it is one that you need not make alone.

How to Use This Book

Most people who worry will have done so for years, so the best advice we can give you is to read this book slowly. Please read that sentence again! Don't read this book all at once—take time over each chapter and do the exercises at the end. Use the Notes pages, or even a special notebook. Discuss the book with a friend. Reread it. . . . You get the point!

This book is designed to be read in the order in which it is written, but if one chapter grabs your attention, then go for it. Your interest and motivation are key factors in your recovery. However, because worry is like a weed, it needs to be taken out by the root. We would like to suggest that you will eventually need all the chapters in this book to do that.

As we've said, each chapter will have some exercises at the end. Please do take the time to do them. If you went to see a physiotherapist, you would expect to do some strengthening work in between sessions. It is the same here. You will not benefit fully from each chapter unless you take the time to reflect and put into practice what you have learned. Things will have to change, and our exercises are basically safe experiments in trying things a new way.

Worry is a real problem for real people, and we have used a number of personal stories to help you understand certain points. These are composites, based on our experience of working with lots of different worriers (including ourselves!)

over many years. However, they don't represent any individual's material, unless specifically stated, as we always respect confidentiality.

If you have a very severe problem with worry or struggle with significant depression as well, we would suggest that you do not read this book alone. Reading this book with a friend, church counselor, or doctor will make your recovery even more likely. Your general practitioner will also be able to help you by prescribing medication or referring you for therapy, if that is appropriate. (See Appendix 1 for more information on this.)

1

Why We Worry

I am an old man and have known
a great many troubles,
but most of them never happened.

MARK TWAIN

When I (Rob) get up in the morning, I tend to do things that I think will be useful. I have breakfast to give me energy. I brush my teeth to keep them healthy. I put on clothes because others will appreciate it! My point is that we tend to do things we believe will have value. So what is there to worry about?

If you ask most worriers, they will tell you that churning away at things doesn't help, but they think it does—at least at a deeper level. There must be something about worry that we think assists us, which means we do actually value it (like our old pair of comfortable jeans) and believe it is useful to us. And so we are reluctant to discard it.

In this chapter, we present worry as a process (or thinking style) with clear patterns and goals. Worry doesn't just happen.

We learn to do it over time, and it tends to operate the same way in different people. It is this that gives us hope, because if we can understand the processes and patterns, then that is the first step to overcoming worry.

Where Worry Starts

Worriers can typically trace their worrying back to childhood, and even to their parents or other family members who worried before them, so there is a genetic contribution to worry that is important to understand.

Psychologists talk about hardwired aspects of our personality, such as whether we are more introverted or extroverted. These aspects are neutral and not illnesses or problems. It is fine to be either an introvert or an extrovert—or even a mixture of both. All parts of the spectrum come with strengths and weaknesses that are well within the normal range, and are fully compatible with living a fulfilled life.

One aspect of personality that psychological testing has repeatedly shown to be part of the normal spectrum is "neuroticism": a tendency to think about things and to be cautious. This has obvious advantages in life: for example, if you are neurotic, you are less likely to be the first one into a fight. But there is also a downside, in that you may be more reticent about going for a new opportunity. On balance, however, it is seen as a valuable aspect of human personality. Evolutionary biologists would say that neuroticism is genetically "successful," that it has been helpful enough to have been selected over many generations. People who score highly on neuroticism scales are compassionate, careful, and make good friends. The other stable aspects of this type of personality are extraversion, openness to experience, agreeableness, and conscientiousness.

Neuroticism is the part of personality that is least talked about. One common personality questionnaire, the Myers Briggs Type Indicator, doesn't even mention it.[1] Instead, it focuses on the other four dimensions above. So why doesn't it measure neuroticism? One explanation is that Myers Briggs was in part developed for business use, and businesses generally don't see the advantages in neuroticism, but love extroverted, open, agreeable, and conscientious workers. The result is that, in our culture, people who tend toward neuroticism are made to feel they are abnormal—even when they are very strong in some respects and well within the normal human range.

> Jonathan thought deeply about things. He liked to see situations well and truly proven before participating in them. He would often be the last person to adopt a certain fashion or fad, preferring to stick with "classic" styles and tried-and-tested ideas. Other people who were always off to the next big thing frustrated him; he thought there were more important things than

the latest iPhone, for example. He placed his focus instead on spending time with people—often people who couldn't afford the fashions anyway. They felt comfortable with him. He sensed that he was connecting deeply with them. His deep thinking meant that he remembered their birthdays and what they had said the last time they had met. They felt understood, but to him, the constant deep thinking caused him worry.

It's true that people who come with this genetic background—the deep thinkers—are more likely to develop problematic worry. But this is only part of the story. Many people with this personality aspect do not worry, and the personality itself is not a problem—it is normal. So it is possible that instead of being problematic worriers, these people may simply be healthily slightly neurotic! However, given the link between neuroticism and unhelpful worry, if you do have a tendency to think deeply and cautiously, you may start to respond too deeply and too cautiously over time, whereas a less neurotic personality might brush things off more easily or not even give them a thought. A good example of this is if you experience a near miss, such as nearly going into debt, or nearly lose a parent to cancer, and you begin to think too deeply. This can lead to you making extra plans and taking extra precautions in the future to try to make sure something never happens again—and then to do a lot of worrying about whether these plans and precautions are enough, or not . . . or maybe they are . . . but then again . . .

Families can also contribute to this excessive thinking. They may live by sayings and mantras such as, "Better safe than sorry" or "You never know." There is truth in these thoughts, to be sure, but there is also the potential to take them to extremes. There are also families where no one seems to worry, so a child feels he or she has to, or where a future divorce is so likely that there is no stable ground to rest upon.

The Reason for Worry

Worry is a normal human emotion, and there are times when it is perfectly right to worry—in fact, it would be odd not to.

> Jackie is a mother whose son has joined the army and been posted to a war zone. She knows she can't not care—this is impossible, not to mention immoral, for a mother. But neither does she feel she can allow herself to consider the possible ultimate consequences. If she were, for example, to contemplate her son being blown up, it would probably destroy her, and, at the very least, she would probably have a panic attack. So she ends up having a good old worry instead. If she is honest, her worry has become a comfort. And other

> moms in similar situations share this worry with her.
> Worry is her "friend" at the moment.

Jackie is not the only example we could give of healthy levels of concern growing to worry. Will and his wife, Louie, nearly lost their second child, Joseph Douglas, during the writing of this book. For seven consecutive weeks, their child was treated in the hospital for a serious breathing problem and a complex MRSA infection. Will described himself during this time as having been "the most genuinely and justifiably worried" he has ever been in his life. Interestingly, he says this felt very different from the sort of worry he normally experienced (and you will hear more about these two types of worry later in the book). Will described the sort of "justifiable" worry he experienced as similar to the anguish of the Prodigal Son's father who watched every night for his son's safe return (Luke 15:20).

Worry also has a protective function, ensuring, for example, that we prepare for possible threats when in dangerous places or make suitable arrangements for retirement or times of ill health. But *worry* isn't necessarily the right word to use here—*acute concern* is a better way of putting it—because there is definitely a healthy process of thinking that is driven by a fear of something bad happening. And frankly, if we didn't worry, we'd be dead.

However, this level of normal worry can easily turn into something else. It can begin to have a more unhelpful function, and we get stuck in cycles of worry. Someone once said that worry is like a rocking chair—it doesn't get you anywhere, but at least it gives you something to do.

But what is a normal amount of worry, and when does worry become unhelpful or unproductive? This is very hard to determine, especially because it is circumstantial—such as in the case of the mother above. But worry is more common than you think. We set ourselves an impossible and unnecessarily high standard if we think we will get to a level of never worrying. Research studies have found that 40 percent of university students worry at least once a day, but people with GAD worry about 60 percent of the day, so there does seem to be a spectrum ranging from what is "normal" to what will result in illness.

The Pain of Worry

The Dutch writer Corrie Ten Boom is reported to have said, "Worry does not rid tomorrow of its sorrows, but it does rob today of its joy." People tend to struggle on through with worry, never really relaxing and never really panicking, and this prevents them from enjoying the day-to-day joys of life. They live in the future and never delight in the moment, which is a gift of God, a "present" to us in both senses of the word. They also tend to keep their worries to themselves, believing that other people would not want to help them or be bothered.

Because they enjoy and share things less, there is a tendency over time to slip into isolation and inactivity. Add to the mix that worriers also give themselves a hard time for worrying, and this makes depression much more likely. Many cases of depression start as an anxiety problem of some kind, and then the mood lowers as negative thoughts and behaviors begin to bite.

Worry also tends to get worse and generalize to other areas. Because many worries are about questions that have no easy or possible answers (more of this later), they tend to lead to more and more questions in an attempt to get to the bottom of the problem—except that no bottom exists. This is when worry really starts to turn into GAD and take up increasing amounts of time and energy.

The Process of Worry

All worriers know that, as soon as one worry is sorted out, another will come along and take its place. It's a bit like cutting the head off a weed—another quickly grows to take its place. So we need to move beyond seeing each worry as an individual problem, and focus instead on the general style of thinking that worriers have.

To get the worry weed out by the root, we need to recognize and change this thinking style. Once again, think of it as being a bit like driving in a traffic jam.[2] This time, instead of focusing only on the car in front of you, focus on the general flow of traffic. Take this illustration further and imagine that it is your job to make all the traffic in a city flow as smoothly as possible; you really do need to get the big picture. To manage a city's traffic, you have to focus on the core issues that affect traffic: different types of vehicles, drivers' strongly held beliefs, rush hours, planned and unplanned construction, and so on. There are many parallels we can take from this analogy to help us with worry:

◆ There are different worry themes that, like different vehicles, behave in different ways. Understanding what your worry themes are, and why you have them (and not others), can be the first step in understanding and then not worrying.

◆ Worry uses tricks, like a stressed driver using a rat-run to avoid a traffic jam. But rat-runs in rush hours rarely work, as everyone else uses them, too. If we can learn the unhelpful adaptations we have made in response to worry, the tricks we think work, and then change them, this can help us drive through life more smoothly and probably more quickly as well.

◆ Worriers have beliefs, such as, "Worrying helped me once and can help me again" or "If I worry about my family, it shows I care." These beliefs are based on truth to some degree, but are likely to have moved beyond being useful to now supporting and maintaining our worry. Gently breaking these rules can free up things a lot, as we realize our beliefs are not always true.

There Is a Future

Matthew worries about lots of things, but his main worry is about whether or not he will perform well at work. He wants to get things just right, so that he will be good at his job and please his parents who worked so hard to put him through school. He feels he owes them something, so he spends some time at the start of each day thinking things through. However, what started as a few minutes of problem-spotting has turned into about an hour of making lists, and lists about lists. Whenever he spots a problem and starts to think about it, he spots even more related things that might go wrong.

Over time, and by using techniques like those in this book, he has been able to sit back and see that, although he worries about many individual things, in general he worries about making mistakes and so letting his parents down. He also realizes that things go better when he looks at the flow of his thoughts. He makes decisions about topics that need a decision, agrees to limit his lists about things that have no solution, and challenges his over-positive beliefs about the benefits of worrying. Slowly, he develops a tolerance of the uncertainty this brings, as he learns that this is a normal condition and he is not making that big mistake he feared.

He also learns that, as he spends less time worrying, he can spend more time enjoying his faith, and so he grows closer to God. He finds that he can please his parents and God without needing to be trapped by having to please them, as they all love him anyway. He still worries—sometimes more than usual—but it doesn't take up an hour at the start of his day, and he can go with the flow a bit more as the intensity is less. Matt's reduced worrying didn't mean things got out of control; it meant that they came under appropriate control.

If you have worried for many years, it can seem as though things will never change. However, there are a number of reasons to be hopeful. This book is based on the techniques of cognitive-behavioral therapy (CBT), the approach for severe worry recommended by the latest scientific studies. Also, we authors have been able to change (more about that later), and if we can change, then anyone can! Even more importantly, we have an amazing God who loves us and loves to help us. And finally, we believe in the healing power of prayer and the community of the local church, and would encourage you all to get as much of both of these as possible.

The old adage of learning the difference between what you need, what you want, and what you worry about what you need is relevant here. God knows what we need! Telling the difference is something we will teach you later in this book. For now, we just encourage you to be hopeful, to read on, and to enjoy.

It's also been our experience that addressing our worry doesn't just make us worry less—it can actually make us more mature people, better appraisers of situations and more compassionate friends. Perhaps even in our worry and our dealing with it, God is working for good.

To Wrap Up . . .

We have looked at the origins of worry in our personalities and childhoods, and considered how worry has important and useful functions, but when severe, worrying can cause us great pain. We have looked beyond the individual concerns to see the thinking process behind worry as the problem, and reminded ourselves that this really can change.

Exercises

To make a change, you first need to know your starting point. These questions will help you clarify why you are reading this book and what you hope to achieve. At the end of the book we will come back to your three answers to the last question below.

The two main questions I have about worry are these:

1. _____

2. _____

I understand worry (circle one):

AGREE—PARTLY AGREE—NOT SURE—PARTLY DISAGREE—DISAGREE

I can see a way of getting better (circle one):

AGREE—PARTLY AGREE—NOT SURE—PARTLY DISAGREE—DISAGREE

I feel trapped by my worry (circle one):

AGREE—PARTLY AGREE—NOT SURE—PARTLY DISAGREE—DISAGREE

If worry was less of a problem for me, then I would

1. _____

2. _____

3. _____

☹️ 😒 🙂 ☹️ 😒 🙂 Notes ☹️ 😒 🙂 ☹️ 😒 🙂

_____

_____

_____

_____

_____

_____

_____

_____

_____

_____

_____

_____

_____

_____

_____

_____

_____

_____

_____

_____

_____

_____

_____

_____

2

Understanding My Worry

Doubt your doubts and believe your beliefs,
but don't doubt your beliefs
and believe your doubts.
JOSÉ M. MARTINEZ

How did you come across this book? Was it after a significant event or at the end of a long struggle? Maybe a friend or relative bought it for you, or maybe you slid it onto the counter in your local bookstore under a copy of a magazine in the hopes that no one would notice? For many of us, there will have been a final awakening to the problem we always had but never acknowledged. For me (Will), the London bombings of 2005 were the catalyst from which I realized my susceptibility to worry; following this, I could acknowledge that my worried thinking had been a persistent presence in my life for some time.

A Bomb Has Gone Off!

I remember walking with my wife along the road toward Paddington Station in London, where we lived, for her to get the train to Oxford. We passed a hastily erected police cordon near the entrance of Edgware Road tube station, but this could have been any other day and any other London cordon. I kissed Louie good-bye and wandered off to my office, positioned due south of the station entrance and opposite the cordon line. As I began to delete my junk mail, a strange sense of urgency came over me. I strode out of the building to my flat nearby, donned my largely unworn collar, and proceeded under the cordon, as if this outfit of black and white were some sort of superhero license to action that would protect me from danger.

I saw a lone man running down the street toward me, his face blackened with smoke but who was otherwise uninjured. He mentioned a scene with injured people, bodies maybe. With a step of trepidation, uncertain as to what was around the corner, I proceeded toward the entrance of the tube. Sirens filled what was an otherwise alarming silence along this usually congested street. I still had no plan, largely because I had no idea of what had happened. The only conviction I had was of the need to be present.

Approaching a small group of police officers, I offered my assistance with a confidence that belied my mere twelve months in ministry. For all my theological training, it was only the most basic of bodily functions that crossed my mind, and tea, hot tea. "Would your officers like to base themselves in our hall, use the bathrooms, and have some refreshments?" I ventured.

Within twenty minutes, some two hundred police, fire, and ambulance personnel filled the small church hall. Somerfield supermarket deposited twenty roast chickens on the table, Starbucks provided a hundred lattes, and Marks & Spencer appeared with trolleys of supplies. I buzzed around the room like a mother hen, trying to look in control and full of compassion at the same time. Cordons now surrounded the area—this had become a small, isolated enclave of activity in an otherwise deserted square mile.

It was only after some thirty minutes that our worst fears were confirmed. This had not been a tragic accident, but a deliberate, meticulously planned assault on innocent human life. What we did not know at that stage was that there were other incidents at other tubes. All phone communication was down, and there was only a confused stream of speculation filtering into our hall.

A burly and exasperated fireman asked me, "Will, have you got a TV we could use?" Finally, I felt helpful! As I ran along the street to my flat, I suddenly vomited on the pavement. Thinking nothing of it, I continued on, returning with a small portable TV under my arm. Moments later, with the tiny screen propped up on the altar, the hundred or so service personnel on their break rotation watched in silent disbelief. We were suddenly connected to other teams on other sites, united in horror at the scale of the attack. And then a bus blew up.

It's hard to express how the atmosphere changed at that point, from shock and stoic determination to deep frustration and anger. Of course, I saw nothing other than incredible professionalism, compassion, and organization from the teams that were present with us over the next five days. But it was the unspoken reaction to violence that permeated the air, and this was something I had no reference for. I just kept on offering to talk, make tea, and rustle bags of potato chips on our overstocked food table.

There were moments of hope in an experience of hopelessness, opportunities to listen and comfort. I appreciated the presence of John and Barry, my bosses, who radiated the love of Jesus in a way I could only aspire to. As the week drew to a weary close, I took my leave and the adrenalin began to subside.

After the Bomb . . .

I had little comprehension of how powerfully I would be affected by this encounter. In many ways, I felt like a fraud, not least when I was awarded a commendation by the Metropolitan Police. I had not actually been into the station. I had only viewed it through the eyes of the brave and worthy men and women whom I had had the privilege to serve. Feeling angry or worried, as I often did in the aftermath of the attack, seemed self-indulgent, and I felt as if talking about what I had done was self-serving and ingratiating.

That summer was not a happy time. I felt disconnected from the people around me, but somehow inside I felt that these emotions weren't justified—I hadn't done enough to feel this bad. Returning to London only intensified these feelings, as well as awakening in me the reality that this terror had inflicted upon our community. I could feel the panic rising like a highland mist on a November morning, barely visible but pervasively cold. My mind struggled to turn it off, but I worried not only about subsequent terrorist attacks but also about more general things in the past, present, and future.

Looking back, I'm not surprised by my panic attacks, although I was surprised at the time. I was refusing to give credence to my feelings. They weren't justifiable, or so I thought. My body was shaking, and my mind was waving a red flag. The invincibility I had felt when I first crossed under the cordon had all but disappeared, and I was very scared.

My inner narrative was both anxious and negative, regardless of the intensity of my prayer life or my attempts to meditate on the Scriptures. "What is all this fuss about? Pull yourself together. Things were worse in the war, you know!" I wonder if I had ever believed that my feelings were justified, long before the bomb even. I had stoically faced bullying at school, believing that I was far better off than starving children in Africa and therefore had nothing to complain about. The bomb was the point at which I began to accept that my feelings were important, regardless of how unjustified I believed them to be. It was also the starting point of a love story.

Not some romance novel episode, but a real story about love. I had known how to love others, even God, just not myself. I believed that I had to be strong, useful, or purposeful in order to be loved and accepted. I worried that being vulnerable would be an unacceptable weakness. But Jesus was now showing me: "My grace is sufficient for you, for my power is made perfect in weakness" (2 Corinthians 12:9). Weakness wasn't to be hidden; it was the place where God's power would be shaped in me!

The journey through this "dark night of the soul" was one of incredible restoration and redemption. In many ways, it was the painful experience of the bomb that finally exposed the deep roots of the worry I had lived with for too long. Recovery wasn't just about getting back to where I had been, but going far beyond that to a place of liberty from the tyranny of worry and fear, a place of peace.

I sometimes wonder if I would go under the cordon again. I can only say an emphatic Yes. Some things can only make sense retrospectively—and this was one of them. At the time, I would have given my right arm not to be in that place of pain, but now I see how God can use even the most traumatic experiences to make us more whole.

Finding My Worry Themes

While worry is a universal experience, it is also a very personal problem. My experiences with worry have been, and sometimes continue to be, painful ones. While we have seen that the actual content of each worry isn't as important as the process or style of thinking that is being employed, it is also very useful to identify one's own worry themes. Identifying your main theme (or couple of themes) can help you quickly label a thought as "just one of my usual worries," and also help predict when you might be about to have a worrying time in your life. For example, if you worry primarily about money, then losing your job is going to be more difficult for you than for someone who worries about relationships, health, or faith.

Worry is a response to potential threats, and so to find our themes, we need to explore things that we find threatening. This might sound like common sense, but very often the genuine threat is actually lurking below the surface of a presenting issue. In this way, the hidden nature of the threat often confuses people and leaves them unsure as to why they are worrying at all.

Emma loved socializing and meeting her friends from church, but every time she began to get ready, she became very worried that she wasn't wearing the right thing. Emma found that the more she looked in her wardrobe, the less certain she became about what she wore and the more anxious she felt. She even had to phone her friend Stacey to check that they weren't wearing the same thing. By the time Emma managed to leave the house, she often felt exhausted. While she was out, Emma found herself checking her clothes and making comparisons with what other people were wearing. On one level, she knew that there was nothing to worry about, but at the same time she felt deeply uneasy unless she was worrying about getting it "just right." As a Christian, she felt such a failure. She had even stuck the following verses on a card on her mirror: "And why do you worry about clothes? See how the lilies of the field grow. They do not labor or spin. Yet I tell you that not even Solomon in all his splendor was dressed like one of these" (Matthew 6:28–29).

We may feel like giving Emma advice about valuing her heart rather than her appearance. Equally, we might be concerned that she has developed a shallow set of concerns and really has nothing to worry about. We could contrast her with people's suffering in poorer parts of the world and tell Emma to get on with her life and be grateful. However, the problem that Emma is suffering from is far more complex than it appears.

Behind many apparently superficial worries lurk far more catastrophic threats and fears. Worriers rarely acknowledge these, as they often don't connect the dots between their immediate concerns and what lies behind them. In fact, Emma was terrified of being humiliated in public. This fear had been generated from an early experience of turning up at a "home clothes day" in her school uniform. Her mother had dropped her at the gates, and Emma had unwittingly walked into a barrage of humiliating abuse. This deeply painful experience had taught Emma that there was a significant threat associated with not looking "right," and that she could stay safe by worrying about her appearance (a worry rule we will discuss later). Her worry was driven by an extreme sensitivity to social acceptance. Her theme was anything that related to her appearance and popularity. She would have deeply loved it to be otherwise, but this was what pushed her worry buttons.

It might seem that your worries are forever changing and different, but it may be that they just seem new. I (Will) run a worry seminar called "Worried? Why?" at Christian festivals Whenever I do this, I always ask people if they have had the experience of déjà vu worry. They are worrying about something that they are sure they had resolved six months ago. Most people will nod their heads as they recall that, while the worry felt new, they may well have stewed on it or something very similar in a previous period of worry. If you aren't finding that any themes come to mind, try keeping a journal for a month and note every persistent worry you have. It won't be long before similarities appear.

Four common areas that people worry about are relationships, finances, work, and health. Christians can also worry about their Christian journey, but we need to note at this point that we are not talking about healthy Christian concerns, but about exaggerated fear reactions to issues of faith. (We will look at these in Chapter 5, "My Faith and My Worry," when we consider why our faith sometimes seems to make us worry more, not less.)

Please note also that a person can have more than one worry theme. Life's hurts are diverse, and many people are carrying unhealed scars that cause sensitivity to a number of different issues. It may be that you will discover that your worries fall into two or three different themes. We suggest you rank them in order of significance, starting with the most distressing.

The good news is that, in dealing with the way we think about one theme, we will develop the tools to overcome our problems with the others, too. Though we can probably deduce an underlying sensitivity for each worry theme, we don't need to remember any trigger event in order to overcome it, so there is no need to scour our childhood memories for that key moment of pain.

Sanjay spent the weekend plagued by the sense that he had offended his mother while on the phone with her. He wasn't sure why he felt so concerned, but she had sounded "off" and "cool" with him. For most of Saturday he stewed about what he had said and how he had said it. Then on Monday night he woke with a sharp pain in his side. He took some acetaminophen, but on Tuesday he started researching on the Internet what it might have been. By Thursday Sanjay was really wound up as well as concerned that people at work would have seen a fall in his performance, and so he worked overtime to assuage the fears that his boss might call him in for a performance review. On Friday he had little energy and started to worry that his girlfriend would think him boring if he suggested they have a night in to watch TV.

If you were trying to help Sanjay identify one or two of his worry themes, what would you suggest: relationships—finances—work—something else?

_____

_____

_____

Threat Avoidance

Human beings are hardwired to get away from threats as quickly as possible. We have a beautifully designed safety mechanism in our brains called the limbic system that operates to alert us to danger and protect us from it. You could say that problematic worry demonstrates the perfect functioning, but inappropriate operation, of this system. Worriers have a limbic system that is extremely sensitive, part of which (the amygdala) tends to fire out threats that are either disproportionate or completely unrealistic.

Imagine that the majority of the population is like tourists in the jungle. They wander around, expecting to see beautiful creatures. When they hear a rustling in the trees or the snapping of a twig, they look expectantly for something nice; sometimes they pay attention, but at other times they don't even look up.

Worriers are in the same environment as the tourists, but they hear every rustling branch or snapping twig as a serious threat to their well-being, perhaps indicating the presence of a ferocious beast or a hungry snake. Worriers are completely unable to dismiss the sensation of anxiety they experience. Their almost instant first reaction is to run away from the threat as quickly as possible. Their brains jump from a stimulus to a complex worry response.

A major part of recovery from problem worry is resisting the urge to run away from fear. Worriers need to stay with the threats they perceive long enough to realize they don't actually pose a risk. By avoiding threats and running out of the jungle too quickly or suppressing the things we are afraid of, we learn nothing new about our thought patterns or how we might respond differently.

Tackling avoidance is essential in overcoming worry problems. This is a topic we will be returning to throughout the book. Understanding our worry themes really helps us to tackle problem avoidance, as it reduces the surprise factor that plays such a strong role in initiating the worry cycle. If we spend enough time becoming threat aware, then our worry response will become much weaker and less persistent.

My (Will's) experience with problematic worry was often very painful. My worries seemed to come out of the blue. I would be reading the newspaper and something would capture my imagination, and I would suddenly be consumed by worry. I often found that when one concern had faded, I would be fine for a while, before another strong worry took over. For a time I might be worrying about my health, then my family, then my friends, and then something else. I would worry about anything that could pose a threat to the people I loved or the relationship I enjoyed with them. I would become agitated if someone was late and often phoned to make sure they were all right.

Having a happy childhood and loving parents made understanding the cause of my worries really challenging. But I persisted in exploring what was fueling my worry. Eventually, it became very clear to me, in part through God's revealing, that I was terrified of being abandoned by, or separated from, the people I loved. If I wanted to be clinical about it, I would say that my worry theme was the threat of abandonment. It was some months after the bomb that I committed to look closely at this area and began to make progress.

I soon found that I was using the process of worry to escape from the threats that appeared in my world. Worry seemed to be a way of working out the problem, but actually, it was the problem. I was using it as a way of running out of the jungle. The fact was that the action of worrying gave the threats greater significance than they deserved, strengthening them and increasing their frequency. It was only when I could identify the theme clearly that I was willing to sit with the threats long enough to see that nothing actually happened!

Getting a "Ready-for-the-Journey" Attitude

If you are looking for a button that will release you from ever worrying again, you will not find it in this book. We have been working with worriers in the church and the Christian world for more than five years now and have met many people who are still looking for an instant cure. Some of them return to our seminars year after year, hoping to find some new way of overcoming worry once and for all. I (Will) have come a very long way in my relationship with worry, but I cannot say that I don't struggle with problem worry at all anymore. However, I would say that it has moved from being a problem most of the time to being an occasional irritation.

It takes determination and courage to overcome worry, and fortunately, worriers tend to have both in large quantities. They have spent years determinedly worrying about things that often don't bother the rest of the population, and they are constantly facing the scariest scenarios that their minds can imagine.

As Bible-believing Christians, we subscribe to miraculous healing, and we are certainly not discounting the fact that God does occasionally heal people of worry issues in an instant. However, in the vast majority of cases that we see, God seems to work alongside our own efforts and intentions. You could ask whether there needs to be healing in a part of the brain that is actually working in a perfectly healthy way, just rather over-sensitively. Perhaps it is more constructive to think about retraining rather than healing, when it comes to overcoming problem worry. Diminishing problem worry can be an uncomfortable journey, but it is also one that deepens our trust in God and increases our confidence that "in all these things we are more than conquerors through him who loved us" (Romans 8:37).

We need to adopt a ready-for-the-journey attitude. Many passages in the Bible encourage us to develop a tough and resilient approach to challenges, being persistent and faithful to God in the face of pain. We, therefore, have a head start in overcoming problematic worry, because our experiences as disciples of Jesus aid us. Remember the promise of Philippians 4:13: "I can do all this through him who gives me strength." This passage is a great comfort when we are trying to make changes in the face of fear, for Saint Paul was in a Roman jail when he wrote it. Consciously lay down your hopes for an instant fix and commit to the healing journey for however long it may take.

Two Types of Worry

Overcoming worry is made more complex because there are actually two main types of worry. We have called them "solvable worry" and "floating worry." Remember that worry performs some important and protective functions in the body, and so we are not attempting to eradicate all worry. What we are trying to do is help you to overcome problematic worry, the sort that steals your freedom and peace of mind. Working out the difference between useful worry and problem worry is central to success.

Imagine you are an art buyer at this point. The art market is flooded with forgeries of an exceptionally high quality. However, they are fundamentally different from the authentic Rembrandt you are seeking to buy. In order to avoid being fooled by the forgery, you need specific training in discernment, training that will enable you to see all of the subtle clues that separate the original from the fake.

This training is especially significant for some Christian worriers, who often find it hard to distinguish between the two types of worry in relation to their faith, again causing incredible amounts of additional anxiety and concern.

1. Solvable Worry

Solvable worry is typically about problems that are currently happening and have a solution that is required now or at some point in the near future. It is often about a clearly understandable problem, one we would all be anxious about. Solvable worry has concrete characteristics and is authentic in that the mind is seeking out a resolution to a problem that provokes appropriate anxiety. The litmus test for solvable worry is that, when shared with friends, they all begin offering sensible suggestions as to how the situation can be overcome.

Solvable worry is important because it stimulates us to seek answers to problems, and with urgency. If one of our children falls ill in the middle of the night with terrible stomach cramps, we may begin to worry about all kinds of things. To solve this problem, we need to give a dose of medication, talk to a medical expert, or look up the symptoms on the Internet—basically, we need to do something, and then the worry will subside.

2. *Floating Worry*

Imagine the scenario we describe above but with a twist. Over a couple of months, your child has two brief episodes of stomachache. You think she is just unlucky with stomach bugs, but then your mind begins to wander. What if it is something more serious, such as a bowel disease, or an underlying emotional problem, such as being bullied at school? Should we take her to the doctor, or would this just be an overreaction, and what if we make the wrong judgment? Despite the ache settling and showing no sign of returning, we continue to worry in a "floating" (or freely floating) way. This is independent of any evidence that would confirm or refute our view, because we are quite capable of making up our own "evidence" in our heads!

Floating worry is not amenable to problem-solving, because it is about problems that do not have answers, and when it comes to sharing them with friends, we generally shy away because we fear that they will think we are worrying about nothing. Floating worry is often oriented around problems that are less urgent and might or might not happen at some point in the future. The level of anxiety is usually less acute, and grumbles along in the background. The worry may be slightly relieved by doing something, but it will come back, because that something we did was not in response to a problem-solving strategy, but to the feeling that we had to do something.

Floating worry examples:

- Maybe I offended that person; they seem upset with me.

- I have a headache again; it must be something serious.

- I can't sense God; I have probably fallen outside his will.

- My daughter hasn't called; perhaps she's had an accident.

- I have hardly any money left this month; I am sure to go bankrupt in the future.

What-Ifs: A Subtle but Important Difference

You can see that, within these two scenarios about the ill child, the events are fairly similar yet fundamentally different. In the first scenario, solvable, normal worry is a useful catalyst for real action in response to a clear and present threat, and if we can channel it, it will make a difference. In the second scenario, the worry issue lingers on, but there is absolutely no resolution. No action is taken other than worry, and the likelihood is that this will persist until another more powerful worry distracts the parent into a different worry cycle.

The best identifier of floating worry is the phrase "What if . . . ?" You can test your worries by applying the phrase "What if . . . ?" If your worries are solvable, it won't work because the issues are immediate: "But I have broken down," "But I have lost my job . . ."

Most people can identify with floating worry from time to time. The key qualification is how persistently and regularly these worries assail you. Problem worry can be identified when floating worry is persistent within the daytime, more days than not in any given week. Problem worriers generally find that the floating worry is present in their minds for more than one hour per day, but Rob and I regularly come across worriers who ruminate on floating worries for hours at a time.

To Wrap Up . . .

Worriers can become very pessimistic about the possibility of changing their habits. I often hear them say things such as, "I have always been a worrier and always will be." Fortunately God is in the business of transformation, and he is very much involved in this process with you.

We have heard the story about how my (Will's) worry developed, and have looked at underlying worry themes that can help us spot the areas that are likely to produce worries within. We have also identified two types of worry: solvable worry and floating worry, which differ in nature according to whether the underlying problem (a) will respond to problem-solving or (b) needs to be tackled in another way because there is no real problem to solve. Now consider these exercises:

Exercises

Using a pencil and paper, group your worries into broader categories or themes.

- Remember that many people worry about relationships, money, and work, and Christians can also worry about sin and their relationship with God. What themes can you identify?

  _____

  _____

  _____

  _____

- As part of this task, you may find it helpful to keep a simple record for a month. Try using this template for a worry diary over a couple of weeks to generate a list of regular worries to consider.

Day	Time	Location	Trigger	What is the worry about?

Some people don't like tables such as the one above, but prefer to keep a journal. However, please use a

> *small exercise book or a page-a-day diary, as this is*
> *meant to be a brief journal and not a novel.*

What one sentence would you use to describe what sort of sensitivity might lie behind these themes?

_____

_____

_____

_____

☹ 😑 ☺ ☹ 😑 ☺ **Notes** ☹ 😑 ☺ ☹ 😑 ☺

_____

_____

_____

_____

_____

_____

_____

_____

_____

_____

_____

_____

_____

_____

_____

_____

_____

_____

_____

_____

_____

_____

_____

_____

_____

3

What Happens When We Worry

> There is nothing that
> wastes the body like worry.
> MAHATMA GANDHI

This chapter looks at what happens in our bodies and our minds when we worry, and the corresponding symptoms. In order to stop a worry cycle from starting, we will look at some simple techniques to control bodily symptoms. You will also learn more about the thought patterns in worry cycles.

Generalized Anxiety Disorder

If you look up *generalized anxiety disorder* (GAD) on the Internet, you will come up with a list of symptoms such as:

- ◆ excessive (out-of-proportion) worry that a person finds difficult to control

- ◆ lack of confinement to a particular problem, but more a tendency to worry

- ◆ accompanied by three or more of these symptoms: restlessness, fatigue, difficulty concentrating, irritability, muscular tension, and sleep disturbance

- ◆ significant distress, meaning that the worrier can no longer perform as before

As you can see, this is more than just a tendency to think on things deeply, which as we've said is part of the normal range of personality. Like any disorder, there are mild, moderate, and severe forms. The more severe forms are likely to need professional help, and this book, though useful, is unlikely to be enough. (In Appendix 1 you will find more information about GAD and how it is diagnosed.)

Michael has always thought about things deeply. He enjoys comments that people make about him being analytical. However, over the past year, there has been a lot of uncertainty at his workplace, and he has had trouble sleeping. He has been tense and jumpy, and this has begun to affect his performance. He has tried really hard not to worry, but this has seemed to make things even worse. He is worried that his boss will notice. He has begun to dislike the job he once loved. He has moved from being a bit of a worrier to someone who has a major problem.

Why Diagnose?

Diagnosis is important for a number of reasons. First, it lets you know that worrying is a common problem, common enough for someone to have given it a name and for us to write a book about it. This is not you going mad; instead, this is one of the ways in which the human brain responds to situations, and help is available. Diagnosis is also important because it can demonstrate to others that this is a real problem and that you cannot simply snap out of it. There is information available that you can give to people (see Appendix 1) and, if the problem is very severe, you are entitled to sickness benefits while you get better.

As we know, mental-health problems are often suffered in silence, whereas physical problems, such as cancer or a broken leg, typically elicit more sympathy. Yet mental-health problems are just as real and, often, just as painful. And many mental-health diagnoses are not lifelong, permanent labels that stigmatize (though some people may use them that way), but rather are descriptions of a problem that lead to a plan for treatment and ideally to recovery.

Worry and the Body

People with GAD usually have at least three out of six bodily symptoms: restlessness, fatigue, difficulty concentrating, irritability, muscular tension, and sleep disturbance. The mind is very powerful and literally controls the body—think of people who get physically sick just sitting in a plane before take-off. However, the flip side is that controlling the body can help the mind. Here we will teach you a couple of simple techniques to help you control your body—how to breathe correctly and how to get a good night's sleep.

Please note that we are not calling these relaxation techniques. We do not want you to try to relax away your worry. Most people who worry try to do that too much already, believing it to be the answer, whereas most things we worry about can't be controlled. However, what we can do is teach you how to understand bodily symptoms, and how to stop a major period of worry from starting.

Think about what happens to the different parts of your body when you are anxious. We have made a list below, starting with the six core symptoms, but you can probably think of others:

- restlessness or feeling keyed up or on edge

- being easily fatigued, even after simple tasks

- difficulty concentrating or your mind going blank

- irritability and snapping at people for little or no reason

- muscular tension, maybe causing a sore back or joints or a headache

- difficulty sleeping: waking several times each night and starting to think and churn

- feeling sweaty on a regular basis

- chronic loose stools or even diarrhea

- often going to the toilet in response to a mere feeling

- fine tremor, even while at rest

- _____

- _____

- _____

There are some other symptoms that people associate with anxiety, such as palpitations, going red, tingling in the fingers or lips, and being sick. However, these are more commonly found in acute panic situations, such as a panic attack or a social crisis. Here we are talking about long-term, background worry that affects the body.

1. Controlling Breathing

Most people who worry chronically tend to overbreathe. The normal rate of breathing is between ten and fifteen breaths per minute, but chronic worriers can breathe twenty or even thirty times a minute. Ask someone to count for you at a time when you are not expecting it. When we breathe too fast, we blow off carbon dioxide—a chemical we need in our blood. You may have been told at school that the role of breathing is to take in oxygen and remove carbon dioxide, and this is partly true, but we are not meant to get rid of all our carbon dioxide. We need to keep a small amount in order to balance the acidity in our blood and keep the blood vessels in the brain working properly. If we chronically hyperventilate, we lose almost all our carbon dioxide and can constrict the blood vessels in our brain, meaning that we feel fuzzy, cannot concentrate, and become more irritable. This is all before we have even thought an anxious thought!

Learning to breathe properly is just like any other muscle activity—and the key is practice. Here's what you do: twice a day, morning and evening, at a time when you are (relatively) relaxed, practice slowing down your breathing. Do not do this at the times when you feel most worried—it is too late then; you won't learn anything useful and it could actually make your problem worse, as you are trying in vain to control your worry.

Imagine that you have hurt your back and been given some strengthening exercises by a physiotherapist. As we said in the Introduction, you wouldn't wait till just before you had to lift a heavy box before doing a few knee-bends. No, you would do them regularly in the weeks and months after your injury. The same applies here. We'd suggest that you practice this for about five to ten minutes twice a day, maybe just after brushing your teeth so that you don't forget. Here are some more recommendations:

- Find a comfortable chair and turn off the radio/ TV (when the kids are at school or in bed).

- Repeat these four steps: breathe in for one second, hold for one second, breathe out for one second, hold for one second. You can use a watch with a second tick; count 1,000; 2,000; 3,000; 4,000 slowly; or imagine you are tracing out the four sides of a square in midair with one finger (see diagram)—whatever works for you.

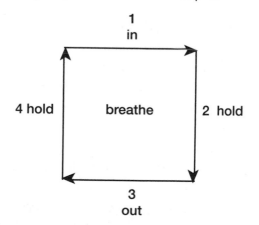

◆ The trick in healthy normal breathing is to observe these pauses between in and out breaths. You will also have noticed that this cycle takes four seconds, meaning that you will take fifteen breaths a minute.

◆ Don't take great big breaths in and out, which would make you hyperventilate. Try to move about a pint of air in each breath. Just breathe with your stomach going in and out, and try not to move your ribs—you can check this by placing one hand on each part. As you breathe in, the hand on your stomach should move out, while the other barely moves at all. Breathe through your nose and not your mouth.

Some people will prefer to use one of the breathing CDs available for purchase. This is fine, but please practice twice a day, and don't wait until a time of stress.

Some Christians worry about breathing techniques that they understand are New Age or Eastern. However, the techniques have been at the heart of personal and spiritual development for centuries, if not millennia. Pop psychology books will tell you that they are at the heart of Buddhism, and so they are, but they have also been used extensively in many Christian traditions, and there is nothing pluralist or occult about them.

Think of the words we use in the Bible for breath: in the New Testament this is the Greek word *pneuma,* and in the Old Testament it is a Hebrew word *rûah.* The Latin word *spiritus* also means "breath." Our ideas of God, spirit, life, and breath are all bound up, perhaps not surprisingly, in the same words, and so the mystics of old used breathing techniques and other types of contemplations to strengthen their bodies and make themselves more receptive to God. Using them to help us in our struggle with worry seems to be a very logical part of this.

2. *Maintaining Sleep Hygiene*

A good night's sleep is one of the most elusive things there is. Yet it is one of the most refreshing things we can have. However, people who worry often start to worry even more if they do not quickly fall asleep.

Chemical methods of falling asleep, such as sleeping tablets, mean that we do not sleep properly: if we are taking them, we don't have enough of something called beta-waves in our sleep, and so don't wake up feeling refreshed. Some sleeping tablets also have a hangover effect in the morning. People may use them for work shifts or jet lag, and although this may be understandable, it is not a good habit to get into. Indeed, your general practitioner should tell you that sleeping tablets are only licensed in most cases for a two-week period. They might be okay for a short time, but ultimately we need to learn how to get a natural night's sleep without them.

You need to start at the other end of the day by establishing a regular waking time, no matter what hour you go to sleep. Try to make this much the same on the weekends as during the week. Next, work at getting the right sleeping environment: make sure you are comfortable, not hungry, in a quiet place, somewhere not too light. Allow a winding-down time before bed, when you stop doing normal routines and do something you only do before going to bed, such as brushing your teeth or reading a magazine.

1. Keep the bedroom for sleeping. The bedroom is for two things only: sleep and sex! Activities such as working, watching TV, drinking, arguing, discussing the day, and so on will make it harder for you to get to sleep. Some people manage these things and then sleep, but if you don't sleep well, keep the bedroom for sleeping and for sex, which can help you sleep!

2. If you wake up for more than ten minutes, or can't go to sleep within ten minutes, get up and go to another room. Stay there till you feel sleepy, and then go back to bed. If you don't sleep within ten minutes, repeat this process until you do. Do not catnap during the day, even for ten minutes.

3. Avoid caffeine after 4 p.m. A small bar of choco-
   late, for example, has 40 milligrams of caffeine. And
   below is a list of drinks and the amount of caffeine
   in a typical cup. As you will see, coffee is not the
   only culprit! Avoid using caffeine as a way of staying awake. (The same applies to nicotine—ciga-
   rettes, gum, and chewing tobacco—as this acts on
   the same receptors in the brain.)

   > Ground/filter coffee: 83 milligrams
   >
   > Instant coffee: 59 milligrams
   >
   > Decaf coffee: 3 milligrams (not zero!)
   >
   > Tea: 27 milligrams
   >
   > Cola drinks: 15 milligrams
   >
   > African cocoa: 6 milligrams
   >
   > South American cocoa: 42 milligrams

4. Also avoid alcohol. Although this can relax you a
   bit, for most people it is something of a stimulant
   and actually raises your heart rate. So, too, does
   exercise before going to bed—it takes time to cool
   down afterward. If you want a nighttime drink, try
   milk with a banana, but not such a big cup that you
   spend all night in the bathroom.

5. If you have babies in the house, this is the time to do whatever it takes to get them to sleep. Ask your pediatrician for advice.

We hope that controlling breathing and sleep hygiene will help you to keep life as free from worry as possible. We would suggest you use them as a regular discipline, as did the believers of old. However, they are also techniques you might want to step up if you know a stressful time is looming, such as going to college or starting a new job, or if you notice that you are beginning to get a couple of bodily symptoms such as muscular tension or increasing irritability.

Martha had heard that a celebrity might be coming to her house soon. She knew that she had a tendency to worry about such things and get flustered, so for the few days leading up to the visit, she practiced our breathing technique morning and evening. She also did her best to avoid too much tea, and therefore she slept better at night. When the celebrity did come to the house, she was still a bit nervous, but she was able to trust that she had done enough preparation and to focus on what he had to say.

Worry and the Brain

We will now look at three common worry cycles, and we'll focus on what we think about when we worry. You will probably be able to see something of yourself in all of them, but we would suggest that you use the one that works best for you.

1. What-If Worry and Vicious Flowers

The minds of those who worry are full of what-if statements, as they think about possible things that might happen next. As we saw at the end of the last chapter, there is a difference between solvable worry and floating worry. The problem with what-ifs is that there is always another what-if you can think of. Brainstorming is a helpful part of cracking solvable problems, but if the worry is about imagined possibilities and is freely floating, then the worry can quickly spiral out of control, and, in theory, anything can be a potential threat. The more you think, the worse it gets.

The illustration on the next page resembles a picture of a vicious flower. The stalk is the first worry, often in response to a trigger. This takes you up to the center of the flower—where you arrive and stew. The result of this is that another worry topic comes into focus. You start to worry about this, but realize that it is probably panicky and unhelpful, so you come back to the center and thus the first petal is drawn. Then another

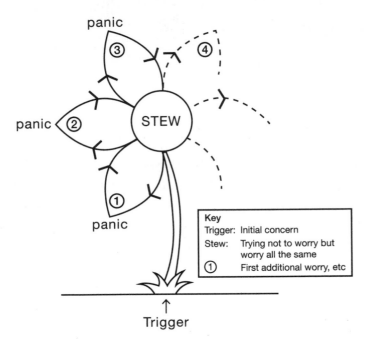

worry topic and another petal . . . and another . . . and another. Eventually there is a full set of petals for your vicious flower. You may stop making petals, but usually only after a few hours or even days and weeks of worry.

2. *The Worry Pendulum*

In the illustration on the next page, the pendulum takes the vicious-flower idea slightly further. It swings from left to right, just

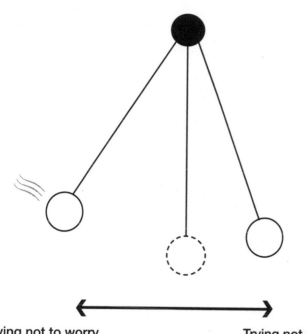

Trying not to worry   **Trying not to panic**

as the worrier stays neither in the middle of the flower nor at the tip of a petal. At the left of the pendulum is "Trying not to worry": the place where many worriers think they want to be, but can never reach. At the right is "Trying not to panic": where your worry might logically take you, but it is very unpleasant, so you avoid it.

Most people can see that the thoughts in the two outer columns in the table are either unhelpfully positive, and adopt a

Trying not to worry	No-go zone	Outright panic
My little boy might be struggling at school. But I have been told he is fine, so I will try not to worry. Everything will be OK. Take some deep breaths.		He might be being bullied, or have dyslexia. He could even be being abused! Oh no, that's terrible. I can feel myself starting to panic.
It's that time of year when people are made redundant, but I'll probably be OK. I really need this job, so I'll have to pray really hard . . . Phew, that's better. Now it is up to God.		If I lose my job, I could lose my house. My spouse will never stay with me. I may never see my children again. My life is over, and there is no going back.

"sealing-over" approach to the problem with some overused platitudes or are unhelpfully negative. However, people who worry tend to swing from one side to the other and not spend much time in the middle. Here there is what we call the no-go zone of half-worry.

The middle is a zone in which people who worry have little experience, because it's a place of uncertainty. Also, they have lots of positive beliefs about worry (so they move to the right) and lots of desires to control worry and remove it (and so they move to the left). This is the main brain model of worry that we will use as we go through this book, and we will be encouraging you to try and spend time in the middle area, to begin to tolerate uncertainty.

3. Worry About Worry

If you have spent a lot of time worrying, you will also be very aware of your thoughts about your worry. You will have worries about your worries (e.g., "How much is too much? How much is wise?"), feelings about your feelings ("Does this feel like the right thing to worry about?"), and layers of behaviors (checking that you are doing enough checking). This is because most people who worry have a fear that they will spiral out of control if they stop monitoring their worry.

However, because most troublesome worries are about possibilities that are vague and ill defined, it is impossible to control these things by worrying, and so monitoring becomes extremely difficult. In fact, it is like trying to herd cats. A huge amount of energy can be invested into worry about worry and about monitoring worry. The extent to which people do this is related to the severity of their worry.

Some experts recommend taking a very close look at these so-called metaworries (worries about worries) and trying to change them.[1] We personally find this quite a complicated and confusing approach. However, it is worth mentioning some of the common worries about worries that people have, as you may think you are alone in having them. Be assured: you are not!

If I worry too much . . .

> . . . will it get out of control?

> . . . will I be unable to think clearly? . . . will I be condemned to a life of anxiety?

> . . . am I weak?/will others think of me as weak?

> . . . does it mean I lack confidence?

These thoughts tend to prolong and heighten worry, thus employing short-term ways of escaping from it, causing the worrier to swing to and fro on the worry pendulum, avoiding the middle ground (i.e., sticking with a worry and seeing what happens).

Worry and Our Actions

We have looked at how worry affects our bodies and our brains, but what do people with worry do? The answer is that they do almost everything they can to avoid getting into worrying situations. If you believe worry to be uncontrollable, you will try to avoid a worry cycle, just as a swimmer avoids a whirlpool.

Worry has many similarities to obsessive-compulsive behavior, which might have occurred to you when reading about the worry pendulum above. Because we are scanning for every possible type of problem, we see lots more problems than the average person sees. We try to avoid problems much earlier on, and the potential problems are more numerous. And we are proactive in searching them out, rather than waiting for them to come to us. You could argue that this is a wise thing to do, but would you really say it was wise to check twenty times that you had locked the front door, for example, or would you say that such rechecking was overcompensation for a pretty unlikely situation?

> Jenny felt her experience with worry was a bit like being in a storm in a boat that she feared was about to sink. She kept throwing life rafts overboard to make sure that, if she ever did fall into the sea, she would probably be near a raft so she would be okay. She could also see that it might be more helpful to spend time and energy keeping the ship afloat by making it face into the wind, and even seeing if she could find a map and navigate her way home. However, throwing the life rafts into the sea was somehow reassuring— she felt as if she was doing something. She also felt reassured when a particular section of sea had a raft in it. Until she saw another gap . . .

To Wrap Up . . .

We have seen generalized anxiety disorder from a doctor's point of view. As a psychiatrist, I (Rob) find this a good place to start. GAD is common and actually fairly well understood—there is hope! We have seen how worry affects the body, the brain, and behavior. We have also seen how we have a love-hate relationship with worry—we don't like how it makes us feel, but we try to keep it under control and so end up oscillating to and fro like a pendulum.

Exercises

We would like you to spend a few minutes reflecting on this chapter:

Do you think you have diagnosable generalized anxiety disorder that is (a) very troublesome or (b) more of a background tendency to worry, i.e., something you find unhelpful and want to change?

_____

_____

_____

_____

How does your worry affect your body?

- ◆ How is your breathing? Count the number of times you breathe in a minute: _____

- ◆ How is your sleep? Think about the last two weeks and make some notes here to refer back to, once you have finished this book.

    Ease of getting to sleep: _____

    Length of sleep: _____

    Number of times waking: _____

Quality of sleep: _____

Feeling of being refreshed: _____

- ◆ How much caffeine do you drink in a day (total cups)? _____
- ◆ What can you do to cut down on your caffeine levels? _____

Which of the three ways of thinking about worry best describes your experience? Why?
- ◆ The vicious flower
- ◆ The worry pendulum
- ◆ Worry about worry

_____
_____
_____
_____

Have you noticed yourself doing things to avoid getting into situations where you might worry? List some of them here:

_____
_____
_____
_____

☹ 😕 ☺ ☹ 😕 ☺ **Notes** ☹ 😕 ☺ ☹ 😕 ☺

_____

_____

_____

_____

_____

_____

_____

_____

_____

_____

_____

_____

_____

_____

_____

_____

_____

_____

_____

_____

_____

_____

_____

_____

_____

_____

4

Worry Fuel:
What Keeps My Worries Alive

When I really worry about something,
I don't just fool around.
I even have to go to the bathroom
when I worry about something.
Only, I don't go. I'm too worried to go.
I don't want to interrupt my worrying to go.

J. D. SALINGER, *THE CATCHER IN THE RYE*

Worry is a problem like an invasive weed with trailing roots, and unless we expose the roots, we won't likely gain freedom from it. Most of us exert our energy pruning worry's top branches, and then find ourselves disappointed that problematic worry has grown back. Here we are going to look at the rules that effectively imprison us in a cycle of worry, and ask what can be done to dig out the underground support of this painful and unhelpful problem.

The Impact of Worry

Once we have been able to identify the fact that we get caught in these destructive cycles of thinking and behavior, it becomes easier to stand back from what is going on and gain a better perspective. I (Will) have often gained comfort from eureka moments in worry when I have suddenly become aware of myself. "Ah," I say, "here we go—I can now make a decision to go down this path and get stuck with this worry, or try something different." However, this is not always possible and it is very rarely easy.

One of the problems that problematic worry causes is that it further damages low self-esteem. Problematic worry undermines our confidence in the things we know are true and leaves us doubtful about our judgments. Worry becomes a style of thinking that provides a faulty, but deceptively reassuring, way to deal with potential threats and challenges. Seventy percent of people who suffer from GAD experience depression at some point, often because worriers focus on negative events and then make negative forecasts about their futures.[1]

> Tom used to feel generally confident. He thought that
> he had good judgment and that he could trust himself.
> However, he was reprimanded by his line manager for
> making a sloppy mistake at work, and his contract was
> brought into question. He became preoccupied with

all the mistakes he had ever made, as far back as his school days. Tom concluded that he was prone to bad judgment, and his self-confidence plummeted. As a result, he then began to double-check his work, scanning and rescanning things for errors. His work slowed down and became more exhausting. When he got home from work, he would again review the decisions he had made, often feeling sick with worry that perhaps he had missed something important. The more time Tom spent worrying, the less confident he became, and the more compelled he felt to worry. Soon Tom began to feel very unsure about his ability to be successful in the long term.

Core Worry Rules

One of the reasons people like Tom struggle with problematic worry is that they have some core worry rules that underpin their worldview. These rules act like the fertilizer that surrounds our worry plant. They ensure that the conditions are always perfect for worry to thrive. Worry rules are the opposite of God's grace to us: they are always absolutes; they are harsh and judgmental in tone and completely inflexible.

A classic example of a worry rule is "I must never make a mistake." What you immediately notice about this rule is that it has some positive value: we would all rather not make mistakes. Christians especially have a tendency toward perfectionism and are extremely scrupulous, not just about their actions but also about their thoughts (more about this in the next chapter). Worry rules often masquerade as attitudes or outlooks that can be helpful, and, as such, we can be very reluctant to challenge them. People view them as choices or values by which to live, and over time they can become embedded in a personality. But if you press these people, it becomes clear that part of them would rather live by another set of rules that leads to less worry.

The first step in uprooting worry rules is actually separating them from helpful beliefs and values (and biblical instruction); here are three characteristics you can use to spot them:

1. *Shoulds, musts,* and *oughts.* Examples are sentences such as, "I *should* be able to do this more easily," "I *must* not show any emotion," and "I *ought* to have done a better job." People go on to worry about whether or not they managed to achieve their goals or, if they slipped up, and whether anyone noticed.

2. *Always* and *never.* Do your friends and family accuse you of seeing the worst-case scenario or the bleakest outcome? These rules are depressive in their content: "Things *never* work out for me/are

always going wrong." They actually drive worry just as much as they drive depression. The classic example is the Puddleglum character from "The Silver Chair" in the *Chronicles of Narnia,* for whom the glass is always half-empty. When told that the weather looks promising, he replies that it will "most likely rain tomorrow."

3. *Consequences—the if-then rules.* If your personal beliefs describe consequences of a particular action or way of thinking, then this is likely to be a rule. An example is *"If* I am very nice to people, *then* I will have lots of friends." Of course, we all try to be nice, but taken to the extreme, this will lead you to try far too hard and to worry if you have been as nice as you should have been.

Yasmin always felt like the slow one in her group. She felt as if her contributions to conversations with her friends were dull or unfunny. Over time she had become increasingly self-conscious and worried about what she might say. It even got to the point where she was reluctant to speak at all. Yasmin resolved that she simply "must not say anything stupid," believing that, if she were clever and chatty, then people would like her more. She was very measured about what she offered in conversation with her friends, and instead waited for a chance to chip in a prepared witticism. Often she would replay conversations in her mind to check that she had been funny enough or interesting enough. Unfortunately, the more Yasmin checked, the less sure she was, and the more worried she became.

As Yasmin became more labored and cautious in what she said, her fears about being slow seemed to be realized more. She started to worry that she would always be boring and would never fit in.

As you can see from Yasmin's and Tom's examples above, worry rules tend to reinforce themselves in a way that makes them hard to overcome. Tom's work deteriorated because of his worry, as did Yasmin's conversational freedom. Underpinning beliefs and associated behavior feed into each other, and the more worrying and checking that takes place, the more realistic the belief appears. India Taylor (from the national UK charity OCD Action) once said, "Some people worry so much about the future, they are in danger of not having one." [2]

Until the sixteenth century, people believed that the world was flat. Sailors from across the globe shared this belief, and held to the associated worry rule that, "if you sail too close to the edge of the world, then you might fall off and die." For thousands of years, this shared worry rule kept people from understanding the truth that the world was actually round, and so they never discovered beautiful and unknown places. It took just one brave sailor, Ferdinand Magellan, in 1519–1522, to demonstrate that the world was in fact round, and to unlock a world of wonder and promise. Worry rules purport to keep us safe or even make us better, but instead they take away our freedom and stop us from learning new and wonderful things about ourselves, our world, and even our faith.

The well-known acrostic "False Evidence Appearing Real" is a very helpful explanation of fear. Until we learn new ways of evaluating our worry rules, we are likely to remain constrained by a fear that overestimates the true dangers we are facing.

Golden Worry Beliefs

Golden worry beliefs not only cause us to become more cautious and worried about specific issues but actually champion worry as a good thing. They suggest things such as "Worry helps me to resolve difficult issues" or "Worry helps me to prepare myself for life's challenges" or "When I worry about problems, they are less likely to happen."

Such golden worry beliefs have been shown to be the greatest obstacles to healing and recovery. Holowka and colleagues have suggested that there are five main types of golden worry beliefs, as listed below.[3] These may prompt you to think about the worry beliefs that you trust in:

1. Worry aids problem-solving.

2. Worry helps to motivate.

3. Worrying prevents things from going wrong.

4. Worry protects from difficult emotions if things do go wrong.

5. Worry makes for nicer people.

We work with people who struggle with substance misuse and addiction. It is clear that, as long as substance abusers have a favorable justification for their addiction, recovery will be very hard. Often, drug users see life benefits from their drugs of choice, saying that using it "gives them confidence, makes them happy and improves the quality of their life." They will find giving up the drug much harder than the addict who actually sees how the drug has ruined his life and stolen his freedom.

You may feel that this analogy is a bit strong, but we want to suggest to you (and we know this from personal experience) that there are great similarities between addiction and worry. It is amazing how many people claim that they are deeply frustrated by problematic worry but on the other hand actually have a partly favorable attitude toward it. It is fair to say that we will never overcome problematic worry if we secretly believe that it is actually helping us out. We have to rid ourselves of all pre-

sumed benefits of worry, just like drug addicts have to rid themselves of presumed benefits of illegal drugs. Beating the habit of
a lifetime begins by seeing it as a problem to be overcome, not
as a friend who helps you.

Reflect Back

Spend some time thinking about your main worry rules and
golden worry beliefs. The best way, if you are able to manage
this, is to ask someone who knows you well to help you identify
them. Ask your friend to be gentle with you, and she will probably be very accurate. You may have thought you had kept your
rules and beliefs hidden, but the reality is that those close to you
will probably know about them anyway. Talk this over with your
friend and write the results below.

My two main worry rules:

1. _____

2. _____

My two main golden worry beliefs:

1. _____

2. _____

A Word of Caution and Compassion for Worriers

We hope that you have been able to identify some core worry rules and maybe even some golden worry beliefs. However, this new information could easily lead you to do one of three things. First, you may say, "I *should, must,* or *ought* not to have all these worry rules in my life; I am so weak/stupid/faithless for relying on them!" Second, you may start worrying that you will never be able to gain freedom from the worry rules that you have identified, and use the classic "always/never" combination: "I will *always* have these worry rules in my life and will *never* be free!" Third, you could be trapped by what change would look like, and think, "*If* I get rid of all these things I believe, *then* I will not be able to cope with life at all."

An essential part of recovery from problematic worry is becoming more aware of the compassionate voice of Jesus and allowing more of that compassion to permeate your own self-talk. Instead of assailing yourself with harsh and critical words, or spiraling into the worry cycle about your worry rules, strive to accept your findings without judgment: "Okay, I have identified some worry rules in my life. Most people will have some of these, and I have done well to find them. It may take time, but I am confident that, with God's help, I can overcome them." We are committed to making this journey with you, which is why we have written this book. (The final chapter picks up on this in more detail.)

So How Do I Break the Rules?

It may seem unusual that a pastor and a psychiatrist might join forces to encourage you to break the rules. This surely isn't the sort of thing that responsible, God-fearing people do! Fortunately, the advice we are giving you isn't about breaking God's rules; it is about breaking unhelpful, often legalistic rules that have kept you hemmed in through worry.

Many worriers are naturally cautious and moral people who hold life's rules in high regard. If they didn't, then they would be unlikely to have a problem with worry. Helping cautious people to adopt healthier and more flexible approaches to life can be a challenge, but we can take great encouragement from Jesus. On many occasions, he challenged the unhelpful legalistic rules that the religious leaders of the time adhered to.

In Luke 13:15, the leader of the synagogue was indignant that Jesus had broken the rules and healed a woman on the Sabbath day. Jesus defended his decision because the alternative, inflexibly adhering to the rule, would have meant that the woman remained unwell. Many worriers remain bound inflexibly to their worry rule, and as a result they also remain unwell.

It is important to remember that we are not expecting you to arrive at your destination in one single step. Overcoming worry is about linking together lots of small steps and changes. Learning to break worry rules is about taking very small steps, exposing yourself to the perceived risk one step at a time, and gaining confidence in the new approaches you are taking. Worry rules become rules by being subtly reinforced over a long period, so breaking the rules will require a bit of careful, gradual, and repetitive unpicking.

Here are three simple ways in which you might be able to rethink your beliefs in your worry rules. (We will deal with the most difficult type, i.e., beliefs about the value of being certain and sure, in Chapter 6. "Tolerating Uncertainty".)

1. Challenge the Weakest, on Paper, First

Undermining one worry rule will have a weakening effect on the others. Pick one from the list you made above that you can immediately see has disadvantages, the one in which you have the least faith. Write it down in the center of a piece of paper. You will be encouraged to know that, by just writing down your worry rule, you will have already weakened its grip on your life.

Focus intently on the rule you have recorded and allow your mind to illuminate how this rule has been impacting your freedom. Pray that God would give you wisdom and discernment in overcoming this rule. Now imagine actually breaking the rule. What would it feel like to have overcome it, and what can you see resulting from your newfound freedom? Don't be too results-focused at this stage; but rather, engage in the exercise for its own sake. These mind experiments can be surprisingly effective; for now, just have some fun in the simulator.

2. Challenge the Logic

This is a good way to work in complete safety on your worry rules. Here we are asking you to think through the logic in your rules and see the inevitable holes and flaws.

We can all be quite concrete about whether something is superstitious or whether it actually makes sense in practice. Let's take a common worry rule and apply some clear thinking: "Worrying about my children's safety will make them increasingly safe." We have specifically chosen this worry rule because, as with many such rules, it holds some distorted rationale. None of us wants to become reckless parents, and all of us have a concern about the safety of our children.

But let's try applying some logic. Think about a common and unfortunate situation: when a child might fall off a bike. Imagine a parent looking anxiously at a girl who is sensibly riding around the playground. Is there anything in the brainwaves of the parent that could be keeping the child on the bicycle? Is the action of worrying creating any special circumstances of safety for the cyclist? Is the sheer act of will making a negative event less likely to happen?

Of course the answer is no. When you think about it like this, it is clear that there is an element of what psychologists call magical thinking going on. We all know that worrying has no preventative power in reality, yet we often hold on to our false belief because it is more comforting than accepting our powerlessness, or even truly trusting God. Sadly, worry is actually stealing the enjoyment of the parent and probably putting the child on edge. If the child does fall off her bike, the parent's worry, or lack of it, has had no influence whatsoever over the incident.

3. Challenge the Benefits

Because we may never have stopped to examine our worry rules critically, we may never have seen the problems they cause. We have believed them to be helpful and beneficial because they are comfortable and familiar. We need to ask, how do I benefit from adhering to this worry rule, and how might I benefit from breaking this worry rule? Putting your worry rule through the benefit challenge gives you a very helpful perspective on the costs of worry and possibly the impetus needed to break it.

In terms of benefits, a worrier who adheres to his rule gets temporary (but partial) relief from feelings of anxiety. He does nothing new, and so remains unchallenged in other areas of life, oblivious to new situations that might bring fresh and welcome information.

The benefits of breaking the rules look a lot more exciting. Although worriers might suffer temporary anxiety, the first benefit is that they are pressing back the encroaching perimeters of worry. They also get to embrace the joy of adventure and the excitement of meeting new people or seeing new places.

Their confidence and self-esteem will grow over time and, even if they encounter difficult things, they can be applauded for having faced the challenge.

Be very specific about what particular benefits this rule is providing for you and what it is denying you. It is often best to do this on paper, using two parallel columns.

Getting Personal

One of my (Will's) personal worry rules that needed challenging was "Worrying that my family members are safe somehow ensures their safety." Obviously this worry rule, like most, was filled with emotion: I can think of few things more important to me than the safety and well-being of my family. On the face of it, this worry rule seems somehow virtuous and healthy, so you can see why giving it up might be hard.

Challenging my own logic was the first step toward overcoming it. The first part of the equation was the connection between worry and my family's safety. I began to think of the things that I did that actually had an impact upon their safety, such as driving sensibly and locking doors at night. There was a clear distinction in my mind between solvable worry issues, such as "The windows are wide open," and floating worry issues which were much more persistent and future-focused: "What if we catch swine flu?"

It became clear to me that thinking a lot of distressed thoughts had absolutely no power to keep my family safe—this was sheer magic. And while I could take reasonable precautions where solvable worry was concerned, floating worry was actually stealing my joy. Adding the whole thing together, it seemed completely laughable that anyone could presume to ensure their family's safety 100 percent without living a completely boring and risk-averse life—even then there are no guarantees!

As a Christian, I further discredited my worry rule by asking who it was who actually kept my family safe. I felt both chastened and confident as I recognized that it was actually God who was looking after us. For example, Isaiah 37:35 says, "I will defend this city and save it!"

I then challenged the benefits of my worry rule. I saw that, rather than making me safer, being preoccupied with worry was making me more clumsy and thoughtless—hardly what I had intended by using it! I also noticed how my anxiety could set my family on edge and prevent us all from relaxing and enjoying ourselves.

Going for the Dragon

One of the greatest moments on my journey to overcome problem worry came at a theme park in Hong Kong when my wife wanted me to join her on a very frightening roller coaster called the Dragon. It had three loop-the-loops and was perched on a very high cliff over the sea. My rigid worry rule about safety led to me upsetting my wife and us leaving the park on a very long and grumpy and much-less-exciting cable car ride. All the way down I subconsciously asked myself if I wanted to live by my worry rule or if I would be willing to break it so that my wife and I could be free to go on the ride. Part of me felt very angry that I was being such a killjoy; the other part was relieved that I didn't have to go on the Dragon!

When we got to the bottom, I grabbed Louie, and we jumped back on the cable car going up. All the way back to the top of the cliff, I felt the usual churning-stomach and sweaty-hands symptoms, but I was resolute that I was going to beat worry, whatever the cost. When we got to the Dragon, I felt full of fear, but I decided that the benefits of breaking the rule were greater than the rule itself. Pulling the roll bar down over my head was scary, and I can't honestly say I enjoyed the ride, but I really loved the sense of victory I had over my worry rule that day. This had a greater impact on my life than I could ever have imagined.

Following Up the Challenges

Challenging our worry rules will increase the flexibility of our thinking. But one of the most frustrating things about worry is that you can't outthink it. Many of us are familiar with the reality that our worries are not rational, especially at 2 a.m. We have to do more than just theoretically discredit worry rules because, without putting things to the test, it is all just theory. We need to take things one step further and change our behavior, just like I did in the Dragon story. If we take action, we will quickly learn that this new way of thinking can be trusted. If you have done the mind experiments above, now is the time to try out something in real life. One CBT principle is "If you want something to change, you will actually have to change something." It might sound as if we are stating the obvious, but you would be amazed at how many people understand their worry rules yet remain constrained by them through inaction.

How you set up and evaluate real-life experiments can get quite complicated, and we will take you through a more structured process in Chapter 6 when we look at challenging false beliefs about certainty. But for now, we just want you to try out some small things. If you are worried about crowds, for example, take a walk to a busy supermarket. If you are worried about illness, go and have a coffee in your local hospital cafeteria. If you worry about safety, head down to the local fair and go on a ride. . . . You get the idea.

Being successful here also means recognizing that our old worry rules are not just going to roll over and die. It is inevitable that we will feel a level of discomfort doing something new, and worry might try to creep in yet again. Our best advice is to feel the feelings but do the feared activity anyway. We can honestly say that, when you begin to instigate behavioral change, your feelings will follow suit quite quickly. But if you back away at the first sign of fear, you will not make progress. The attitude is "I feel afraid—yes! Bring it on—that means I am doing things right!" This might sound a bit blasé, but for most of our worry rules, it boils down to something this simple. These days if you show me a roller coaster, I will be the first on it, not because I love the ride, but because it symbolizes the fact that I refuse to be bound by my worry!

Becoming a Worry Revolutionary

One of the great things about Jesus was that he was a revolutionary, and he calls us to be revolutionaries, too. The revolution he brought wasn't the one that the disciples had been expecting, of overthrowing the Roman occupation in Israel. Instead, he brought a revolution of the heart, a complete paradigm shift in the way in which people could meet with God. All of the teaching Jesus offered was tinged with the language of revolution, of ushering in the kingdom of God. He claimed to have come "to proclaim freedom for the prisoners and recovery of sight for the blind, to set the oppressed free" (Luke 4:18).

Many people are imprisoned and oppressed by worry rules, but we believe that Jesus wants them to be free. For worriers, there can be few better places to start a personal revolution than in their place of great anxiety, a place where Jesus is present. As you follow the exercises in this book, you will notice what

Thomas Aquinas called "corporeal action," the action of God and humankind in partnership as he works for your freedom alongside you. Overcoming worry rules is a challenge where you must lead, but you undertake it with Jesus, reliant on his comfort and encouragement. Like any good trainer, God wants your spiritual and emotional muscles to grow, so he won't be lifting the weights for you, but he will be with you all the way.

Go on, you can do it!

To Wrap Up . . .

We have looked at the main types of worry rules (and golden worry beliefs) and the language that enables you to identify them. We have seen how to put worry rules to the test and reinforce our new flexibility with action. Many worries will respond to simple techniques—it is just that they have never been tested before. We have seen a personal example of how a worry rule was broken, and encouraged you to be revolutionary in your outlook. This is hard and scary work, but definitely worth the effort. Remember that God is working with you through the process.

Exercises

Rewrite the two worry rules you wrote about earlier in the chapter, and then add any others you can think of. (Remember, they are core rules characterized by words such as *should, ought, must, never, always,* and *if . . . —then*):

1. _____

2. _____

3. _____

List the two golden worry beliefs about the positive value of worry that you wrote about earlier, then add any others you hadn't written down:

4. _____

5. _____

6. _____

Write here what you found when you did a mind experiment with your weakest rule:

_____

_____

_____

_____

What logical flaws did you find?

_____

_____

_____

_____

What are the benefits of breaking some of your rules?

_____

_____

_____

_____

What one thing did you learn from Will's example?

_____

_____

_____

_____

We hope you have been able to break some rules. If so, what does it feel like?

_____

_____

_____

_____

☹ 😑 ☺ ☹ 😑 ☺ Notes ☹ 😑 ☺ ☹ 😑 ☺

5

My Faith and My Worry

Pray, and let God worry.
MARTIN LUTHER

A well-known Christian leader, J. John, e-mailed me during the writing of this book, saying that he thought that "Do not worry" was the single hardest instruction in the Bible. I agree. Over the past five years, our work in emotional health has brought us into contact with many, many Christians, and by far the most common emotional-health problems we see in churches are worry (or anxiety disorders) and depression. An often-quoted statistic is that one in four people will suffer from a mental-health problem at some point in their life, and this statistic is no less true for the Christian community.

Many church leaders we've encountered confirm that worry is a problematic, but often unaddressed, issue at the heart of their communities. They also concede that the church is often ill equipped to deal with the issue of worry and other emotional health problems. One unfortunately worded church notice board church notice board read, "Don't let worry kill you—let the church help!"

The Elephant in the Pew

Unfortunately, Christians often anticipate condemnation—not grace—if they reveal that they are worriers. Those with a predisposition toward worry can suffer from an inappropriately strong sense of shame relating to personal inadequacy, compounding their unwillingness to seek help. Hence, many in our church congregations are struggling in silence.

However, the issues that face worriers in church are not purely internal; they originate from the external culture, too. There is a need for all of us to examine the culture that surrounds emotional-health issues in our fellowships, because the latter will either help to reinforce the problem or release people from it. There are "worry rules" that exist in church culture which, while not biblical, give the impression that being worried is proof of a weak or shallow faith. Obviously, a worry problem is compounded if a Christian believes that by being worried, he or she is offending God or expressing a lack of faith. Below is a genuine letter that we received from a Christian about his experience with worry in church:

Dear Mind and Soul, I wonder if I could ask you a question about something that has been bothering me regarding what some Christians have said to me. I've had a lot of Christians come up to me and say things like, "God doesn't want us to be anxious; he's created us for freedom," or "The Bible says do not be anxious over anything," or even better, "If we are not living in joy, it's because we aren't resting in the Father's arms and accepting his fatherhood over us."

I've really struggled with some of these comments, which have either been preached to me or passed my way during my illness. I've known the loving arms of God as my Father for many years, and yet I've had this illness, and it's led me to feelings of guilt sometimes. I know that isn't right either, but I just feel uncomfortable with what some people are saying, and I don't believe it's all as simple as they're preaching. What's the correct response as a Christian to the comments I've received?

The Bible has a lot to say about worry, and not all of it is easy to digest. However, we believe that "all Scripture is God-breathed" (2 Timothy 3:16), and that nothing should be discounted because of its complexity. What you will notice from the letter above is that problems arise not so much from the biblical texts, but from the insensitive way in which some Christians offer advice. In this next section, we are going to look at the key biblical text about worry, before we go on to see the centrality of faith in Christ and the community of the church in healing.

Worry in the Bible

There are very few references to worry in the Bible. Only one reference to worry can be found in the Old Testament, and of the eleven New Testament passages, seven come from two parallel passages in Matthew (6:25–34) and Luke (12:22–34). Matthew 6 perhaps best encapsulates Jesus' teaching on worry, and it is through this key text that we hope to help you continue on your journey to freedom:

> Therefore I tell you, do not worry about your life, what you will eat or drink; or about your body, what you will wear. Is not life more important than food, and the body more important than clothes? Look at the birds of the air; they do not sow or reap or store away in barns, and yet your heavenly Father feeds them. Are you not much more valuable than they? Who of you by worrying can add a single hour to his life?
>
> And why do you worry about clothes? See

how the lilies of the field grow. They do not labor or spin. Yet I tell you that not even Solomon in all his splendor was dressed like one of these. If that is how God clothes the grass of the field, which is here today and tomorrow is thrown into the fire, will he not much more clothe you, O you of little faith? So do not worry, saying, "What shall we eat?" or "What shall we drink?" or "What shall we wear?" For the pagans run after all these things, and your heavenly Father knows that you need them. But seek first his kingdom and his righteousness, and all these things will be given to you as well. Therefore do not worry about tomorrow, for tomorrow will worry about itself. Each day has enough trouble of its own.

These verses act as a piece of divine cognitive behavioral therapy (CBT). Jesus is challenging us to be transformed in our response to perceived threat, and to find new and true ways to face life's challenges.

A Command Not to Worry

Jesus actually commands us not to worry in verse 25. This has caused a lot of anguish for Christian worriers, but in many ways we should find it deeply reassuring. Can we imagine Jesus saying anything else? If Jesus advocated problem worry, what would it say about his relationship with the Father? His teaching on worry correlates emphatically with his understanding of God's power. It is precisely because God loves us that Jesus commands our trust. The Christian gospel is good news because it offers the complete restoration of the father/child relationship between God and us. Jesus is challenging us not to remain independent of him by incessantly worrying about our own needs. He calls us to be God-reliant, to know that he cares for us and will provide all that we need.

Does That Mean We Should Do Nothing?

The King James Bible (Authorized Version) translates verse 25 in a different way. It says, "Take no thought," suggesting that Jesus is commanding us here not to give any thought whatsoever to our futures or needs. Consequently, some church cultures imply that, like the birds (verse 26), we should sit on a branch and wait to be fed. But, as Dr. Martyn Lloyd-Jones points out in his commentary on this passage, birds and humans have very different ways of getting food: birds wait for new shoots to appear, but we have to till the ground and sow the seed![1] To have faith in God does not mean sitting around with spectral light on our faces waiting for manna to fall from heaven, any more than awaiting his return involves heading for a log cabin in the mountains to sit out the last days. Jesus is challenging us, not to give up all concern for food or water or clothing or other things we need, but to give up an insightless, faithless obsession with security.

An Obsession with Security

Jesus teaches us not to "run" after the certainty of provision (verse 32). The commentators translate this verb in various ways, including "pursue," "search," and "seek after." All of them suggest a level of desperate obsession, but in my opinion, the best word is "run." To Jesus' first-century audience, the idea of running was disgraceful and improper. It showed that a man had lost sight of himself and his dignity. It is part of the reason why Jesus' other teaching of the Prodigal Son (Matthew 6) is so powerful. Jesus makes a distinction between running desperately after things and a trusting awareness that "your heavenly Father knows that you need them" (verse 32).

In this book, we are calling you to see problem worry and its rules and behaviors as a fruitless pursuit of an impossible certainty. Striving for certain security is not just irrational and fruitless; it undermines the very nature of God's good character.

Our Ultimate Goal

The key verse of this passage and our ultimate goal is verse 33: "But seek first his kingdom and his righteousness, and all these things will be given to you as well." The next verse appears to read like something of an anticlimax: "Therefore do not worry about tomorrow, for tomorrow will worry about itself. Each day has enough trouble of its own" (verse 34). However, this final verse is in fact an important CBT tool that helps us to get to the kingdom-seeking place referred to in verse 33. Let's now unpack verse 34 in more detail.

Two Types of Worry—Today and Tomorrow

Jesus does not offer impotent advice, such as, "Try not to worry" or "Maybe it will get better in the future." He offers powerful instruction that makes for real and lasting change. In verse 34 he deals with two types of worry: that of today and that of tomorrow. You will see immediately why we have been talking about two types of worry in this book: because they tie into these two time frames. The two types also happen to be highly recommended by modern psychology, but for us that is secondary to the fact that it is the wisdom of the Lord!

◆ *Today has enough trouble of its own (verse 34b)*. Be clear with yourself about what are the solvable worries that you can deal with today (and you'll learn problem-solving techniques in Chapter 7, "Taking Action").

◆ *Tomorrow will worry about itself (verse 34a)*. Identify the floating worries—the hypothetical what-ifs about tomorrow. Commit not to try to solve them, but use a technique called Christian present contemplation or contemplative prayer (also taught in Chapter 7).

Jesus leads worriers out of bondage by leading them into the now. He asks us to learn to focus on the present (the now and the gift) of the good news of the kingdom of God. Learning this focus takes time, and we will essentially spend the rest of this book teaching you how to do that. Once you become better able to retain a focus in the present, you will notice an increase in your ability to trust Jesus and find deeper peace.

The Kingdom Lid

When we seek God, as a present action (verse 33), we find three things: the kingdom, his righteousness, and all the other things.

First, worry needs a lid to keep it from spiraling out of control, and the kingdom is a lid on all our concerns, for there is nothing higher. Once we have stopped running after security and started to focus on the kingdom, the latter maintains our perspective and also keeps us from seeking another way of living, one that is anxious and worry provoking.

Second, God's righteousness is not a focus that brings condemnation, but rather a reminder that it is his righteousness that sees us to heaven and not our own. We see that God loves us and has made a way for us. As hymn writer F. J. Crosby famously wrote, "Blessed assurance, Jesus is mine." Only through the death and resurrection of Jesus Christ, and the forgiveness he offers, can we truly know righteousness. If we take action both to seek first the kingdom and put our faith in Christ, then the third promise of "all the other things" is at the same time both awaited and often not needed. Faith is restored.

Applying the Teaching—The Problem with Certainty

Much of Christians' discomfort with worry relates to issues of faith and certainty. Worriers, by the very nature of their disposition, earnestly seek to be certain that everything will work out okay. Unfortunately, many Christian worriers sense that they are subject to God's anger first and his grace second, and they become preoccupied by specific faith worries, anticipating that everything won't turn out okay after all.

A question from a Christian website is a classic example of the problem of uncertainty and faith:

> I would just like to know if what it says in the book of Matthew is true. It states that every sin is forgivable, except if a person speaks badly about the Holy Spirit. I attended a private Christian school, and one day my Bible teacher was saying that a person will not be forgiven if he/she speaks against the Holy Spirit. As he stated that, I thought something against the Holy Spirit. I did not mean to . . . it just happened. I prayed and asked for forgiveness, but does that mean I am forgiven or eternally condemned? Sincerely Worried

Sincerely Worried is not alone. There are literally thousands of sites offering consolation to Christian believers who are uncertain as to whether or not they might have committed the sin recorded in Matthew 12:31 and Mark 3:29. This is just the sort of thing that illuminates the faulty thinking that surrounds problematic worry. Having heard of the existence of a potential threat to his relationship with God, Sincerely Worried automatically thinks of the thing that would identify him as guilty, and then proceeds to be convinced of his guilt. In many ways, he is no different from the person who hears about a rare disease and then begins to believe she has contracted it. Or the person who tries to think of anything but a pink elephant—and the pink elephant appears. . . .

In Mark 3:29 we read: "But whoever blasphemes against the Holy Spirit will never be forgiven; they are guilty." What does this actually mean? In these parallel passages, Jesus is accused of using satanic force to drive out another evil force and points out the ludicrous nature of this accusation. He also tells the people quite squarely that, if they ever again attribute his power (which comes from the Holy Spirit) to Satan, this would be unforgivable.

The reason this has eternal significance is that it is impossible both to reject and defile the name of the Holy Spirit while also seeking forgiveness and salvation from the same Spirit. You can't try to climb into a lifeboat at the same time as you say that you don't believe in boats! Also, repentance is itself a spiritual gift (see Acts 5:31 and 2 Timothy 2:25), so the Holy Spirit is unlikely to be giving you something and taking it away at the same time.

Two pieces of advice are usually given to Christians who worry that they have committed the unforgivable sin. The first is theological: we can study the context and see here that Jesus is addressing leaders. Furthermore, the whole of the Gospels is good news and not an accusation against men and women. We can also look at the dialogue and see that what really gets to Jesus is a public, clear, and deliberate statement that his power is satanic, whereas the worrier's fear is typically covert, unsteady, and resisted with all his might. If you are a Christian, you are filled with the Holy Spirit, and so by definition have not rejected him.

The second piece of advice is psychological. If you are uncertain about having done something, then the chances are, you have not done it, and it is the feeling of uncertainty that is causing you to worry. Seeking to fix the problem by checking or double-checking only compounds uncertainty. Consider Tamsin:

> Tamsin found herself in an unbearable loop. She knew something of the love of God and had put her trust in the forgiveness that Jesus offers her through his death and resurrection. However, she found herself wondering if she really was forgiven. Tamsin spent a lot of time thinking back over each day, trying to confess every mistake to God and ask for his forgiveness. But how could she be certain of her pardon? Unfortunately, the more carefully she thought about it, the more unsure she became as to whether or not she had confessed everything. She often came to the sudden realization that she was worrying about being forgiven, and was therefore committing another sin that she must confess, so the whole process began all over again.

Mr. Sincerely Worried and Tamsin are not unique Christian worriers; in fact, their problems with certainty are the most common faith-related worries that we come across. The challenge for people like Tamsin is that worry tends to lock on to the things that are most important to us: our health, our family, or our faith. To most Christian worriers, the assurance of God's forgiveness is of paramount importance and an absolute beacon for their concern.

Tamsin has become quite legalistic about her faith in an attempt to find certainty, so that she can relax into her relationship with God. Many worriers are enticed by the feeling that if they could just say one additional prayer, or recall one incident fully to confess it, then they would be certain that everything was going to be okay. Sadly, as we have seen in the preceding chapters, the feelings of worry do not always relate to legitimate concerns, and therefore the feelings of peace are short-lived before fresh new doubts come to mind.

But the theology of forgiveness is based on faith and trust, not on actions and certainty. Until Tamsin makes a conscious decision to stop locking God into a mechanism of forgiveness, and trusts in his love and compassion, she will continue to pour all her effort into this frustrating cycle of doubts and confessions.

Certainty as Impossible

It is not hard to understand why worry is such a problem in the examples above. Christianity is established in the corridor of faith and not certainty. As a friend of ours says, "This is why they call it the Christian faith and not the Christian obvious!" It is possible for you to double-check that the front door is locked (although we wouldn't recommend it) or ask for a second opinion from your doctor to see if a rash is serious. However, there are no such tests for salvation; we can only place our trust in Jesus.

Before Martin Luther gained a new understanding of faith at the time of the Reformation, it is recorded that he was so racked with guilt that he used to roll in thorns to punish his body. He was willing to do all sorts of things to himself because he didn't feel forgiven. Problem worriers often struggle because they don't feel forgiven, or they don't feel close to God, or they don't feel certain. Recovering from problem worry sometimes requires the insight and the courage to believe Scripture over and above what we may feel to be true.

Knowing you are forgiven by God is a combination of reliance on the promises of Scripture, trust in the benevolent character of God, clarity of conscience, and a permeating faith in Jesus. There are no tests that you can take to overcome the nature of faith; in fact, we are actually commanded not to try to put the Lord to the test (Luke 4:12). The wisest thing we can do is to stop seeking certainty.

Certainty as Unwise

We have discussed elsewhere how seeking reassurance is psychologically unwise, as it will fuel your worry in the long term and prevent you from learning any alternative perspective. However, it is also spiritually unwise. The apostle Thomas (with whom we feel a great affinity) moved from doubt into certainty when he placed his fingers into the wounds in Jesus' hands. Yet Jesus told him in John 20:29: "Because you have seen me, you have believed; blessed are those who have not seen and yet have believed."

Being too certain can also affect our faith. The first attribute of God described in the Bible is creativity: "In the beginning God created . . ." (Genesis 1:1). If we are made in God's image, then surely we are meant to be creative, too, and this will never happen if we know the outcome of things before they occur. In some ways, repetition of what is safe and known is the opposite of creativity, which is what led German psychotherapist Erich Fromm to say, "Creativity requires the courage to let go of certainty."

The Search for Certainty Creates Desperation

Most Christian problem worriers find themselves drawn toward desperate attempts to attain certainty. These can lead to unorthodox and superstitious actions, such as creating tests for God based on the Gideon fleece principle (Judges 6:36–40) or using the Bible as a fortune-telling device by flicking the pages for a verse. It can also lead people to try to acquire the man-made trappings of religion, such as a title or role, or seeking a specific gift or special authority.

Unfortunately, all of these things further confuse how we should relate to God as Father. Imagine someone you loved coming to you with a series of tests that proved your love for them. How would you feel? If anything, rather than confirming the integrity of the relationship, these would bring further uncertainty. The paradox of any search for certainty is that it invariably creates the opposite sentiment: doubt! There is another way: the huge value of Christian contemplation, which we will discuss later in this book (in Chapter 7, "Taking Action"). In this we do nothing other than be present with ourselves and present with a God of love. It is an amazingly effective treatment for overcoming problem worry.

Church Is Part of Your Healing

As a church leader, I (Will) am passionate about the role of the church in healing people who suffer from problem worry. I am also encouraged by the aspirations of leaders across the spectrum of church tradition who long for their church to be a place of healing and release. While there are instances where the church culture may not be as emotionally attuned as we would like, in the vast majority of cases, the church is already having a profoundly positive effect upon people's emotional, spiritual, and mental health. If you are a leader reading this book, we want to thank you for all that you are doing to love and support your congregation on their journey to freedom in Jesus' name.

As the body of the church, all of us have to take responsibility for creating a culture that is rich in God's grace, and where biblical wisdom regarding worry is married to practical application. If the wisdom is "Perfect love drives out fear" (1 John 4:18), then it is our corporate responsibility to help worriers use the perfect love of God in the face of persistent fear. This may involve ongoing prayer, practical support, Bible study, counseling, ministry, discipleship, and most essentially, unconditional love. We need to be great at saying, "This wisdom works, and God wants you to find greater freedom. However long it takes, I want you to know I am walking with you. Feel no shame, for Jesus is here."

Christian worriers (like ourselves) also impact the *culture* of healing in the church. We need to apply biblical wisdom with tenacity and determination. It can be easy to fall into defensiveness as a worrier, for this is the essence of the problem: worry is pre-emptive self-defense. If we are told, "Perfect love drives out fear," then we can easily hear, "If you really knew the love of

God, you wouldn't be afraid!" even when this was not actually intended. We must be skeptical about our defensive tendencies and celebrate the good intentions of our church family in their desire for our healing. We need to continually choose to believe the truth and engage with it. We need to be tenacious in ensuring that our application of the Scriptures is actually helping to fulfill one of their intended messages: worrying less. And it is important to remember that this will likely take patience, determination, and persistence.

To Wrap Up . . .

We have carefully examined Jesus' key teaching on worry in Matthew 6, and found that our faith is not only comforting news but also dynamic medicine for worry. We have considered how certainty and faith are incompatible, and looked at some of the specific problems that Christian worriers struggle with. We have identified the two types of worry in Jesus' teaching and set out a completely fresh approach to floating worries. We have seen that the church and its community play a fundamental role in our recovery from problem worry.

Exercises

What has held you back from wanting to talk about problem worry with Christian friends or within the church?

_____

_____

_____

Read Matthew 6:25–34 at least three times out loud. What are your thoughts?

_____

_____

_____

How connected do you feel to the love of God? What in this chapter has most helped you in this area?

_____

_____

_____

What have you decided about the quest for certainty in issues relating to your faith?

_____

_____

_____

☹☺☺ ☹☺☺ **Notes** ☹☺☺ ☹☺☺

6

Tolerating Uncertainty

Uncertainty is the only certain thing there is.
PLINY THE ELDER, AD 79

One old hymn says, "On Christ the solid rock we stand; all other ground is sinking sand." We love to be certain about things; it makes us feel safe and comfortable. However, as you are learning in this book, there are many areas of life about which it is impossible to be certain, the Christian faith being one of them. Yet we still value certainty highly, and to some degree, we despise doubt.

In this chapter, we will build upon the "worry pendulum" illustration (page 61), where we swung between "trying not to worry" and "trying not to panic," and then spend some time learning how to stay in the middle area. This might seem like sinking sand when you first try it, but actually it is the most solid place to be.

The Roots of Uncertainty

Harriet found a small lump on her shin while putting on some sunscreen at the beach. She went to see her family doctor. He prodded it and said it was almost certainly the result of an old injury that had become calloused, and there was nothing to worry about. If she hadn't been to the beach, she probably wouldn't even have noticed it. However, "just to be on the safe side," the doctor referred her to the hospital for an X-ray and an appointment with an orthopedic surgeon.

Initially she felt better, but that evening her Internet search didn't help—she found stories of bone cancer and worse. During the time before her hospital appointment, which was three weeks away, she swung between tears and more frantic searching on the Internet while trying to get on with life and look after her three children. She prayed urgently, then told herself not to overreact.

Harriet had some insight into her condition, but really she wasn't sure what to do or how much she should be worrying. This in itself became a worry, so she was even more worried about whether or not she was handling it properly.

The doctor's aim was clearly to reassure. However, worriers are supersensitive to even the smallest amount of uncertainty and have an ability to make a molehill into a full-fledged mountain very quickly. This story also shows how ineffective reassurance can be—it may work for a while but it will never remove the uncertainty 100 percent, and so will not keep the worrier happy for long. It also shows how ineffective worrying about worry is, and how it makes the worry worse overall. This is why we need to learn to *deal* with uncertainty rather than trying to *remove* it.

Let's take a moment to remind ourselves of the pendulum. People tend to avoid the extremes because they have positive beliefs about worry and dislike the unpleasant feelings and emotions that come when they worry too much. However, the constant swinging of the pendulum means they keep passing the middle zone—at high speed!

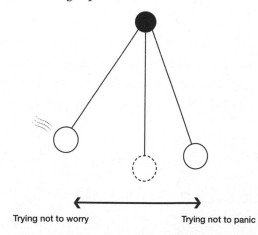

Trying not to worry   Trying not to panic

Trying not to worry		Outright panic
Positive beliefs about worry drive me away from the left. I can't "not worry."	No-go zone	Unpleasant feelings of anxiety drive me away from the right. I dislike "panic."

We also said that this was fueled by "worries about worries" and worry rules, and most worriers will spend quite a bit of time thinking about their problems because they have a fear of losing control, being condemned to a life of anxiety, and being thought of as weak.

Beliefs About Uncertainty

In the same way that people who worry have unhelpful positive beliefs about worry (golden worry beliefs), they also have unhelpful beliefs about certainty. They maintain worry by setting such high standards for certainty that they are quite unachievable. Some of these beliefs are summarized below. Which of these do you have?

- Being uncertain is an unpleasant experience.

- You should act only when you are absolutely certain.

- Better safe than sorry.

- I can't be safe when I am not sure.

- If I am sure, then I can predict bad things and so prevent them.

It may be that these beliefs have arisen from upbringing or personality type or a near miss, but they have grown legs and taken up key positions in the worrier's life. Because they result in such a storm of thinking, aiming to control the uncertainty, they undermine confidence even more—and lead to an even greater desire to find that elusive rock of control, and so become self-reinforcing.

Building Toward the Best Techniques

As you have seen already, we often have to take incremental steps toward freedom from problem worry. The concept of incremental-step training is made clear in sports. I (Rob) used to row quite seriously, but I couldn't simply jump into a top racing boat before I had spent some time in a glorified bathtub floating around on a pond. My work on simulators, in more stable boats and in the weight room, all contributed toward me being able to row well in the "gold standard"—a racing crew.

In the next section you will see that we are building toward the gold-standard technique for overcoming worry: what we call present contemplation. However, this can be hard to achieve directly—you can't just jump into the racing boat—so we are first going to introduce you to two lesser techniques ("thought records" and "making new appraisals") that will help you build toward the most difficult, but most effective technique: "present contemplation." We'll also point out some unhelpful techniques to avoid.

Thought Records

Keeping a thought record is a helpful early training technique that is advocated by many of the best CBT practitioners. There are many different forms in circulation, but the one we are going to show you is the seven-column thought record, described by Christine Padesky in *Mind Over Mood*.[1] Using thought records will help you to identify a troublesome thought, list the evidence both for and against it, and then come up with a more balanced thought, which usually makes you feel better. Your key work here is not to become reliant on thought records as a technique for overcoming worry, but to become much more familiar with your worry thoughts and their irrationality. This technique will also make the link between thoughts and feelings very clear to you.

Creating the Thought Record

There are no actual rules on how to create a thought record, although some people draw out columns, some just use journals, and others use pictures or doodles. The key thing is that you do what works for you in terms of creating a format that allows you to compare and contrast thoughts and moods. For simplicity's sake, we are going to describe it in column form here:

To begin the process, write down the problem worry at the top of your page, trying to be as succinct as possible.

Column 1: Situation. Identify a moment when you had one of your first worry thoughts. It might have been in response to reading something in the paper, something someone said to you, a look from a person, or just something that came while you were daydreaming.

Column 2: Mood. Identify your mood in relation to the worry thought and describe it as simply as possible: angry, depressed, anxious, empty, on edge, despairing, or whatever. Rate your mood out of 100.

Column 3: Automatic thoughts (and images). Write down any automatic thoughts or images that arise as a result of the worry thoughts that pop into your head. If you were worried that you were getting ill, you might have the thought, "I am going to die." If you were worried about losing your job, there might be a vision of being homeless or bankrupt. Pick one of these thoughts and highlight it as the main worry you want to work on.

Column 4: Evidence for. Identify and write down the evidence that supports the likelihood of your worry coming true or being true. If this evidence is concrete, it may indicate that you are facing a solvable worry and can use problem-solving techniques to overcome it.

Column 5: Evidence against. Write down any evidence that opposes your worry thought. Look for rational or factual points that either refute the worry or lessen its significance. It may be that this process enables you to identify that the problem is simply floating worry, and that you can use the techniques we are teaching you to overcome it.

Column 6: Alternative thoughts. Review your original worry in the light of the evidence you have just considered. Try to create a thought about the issue that takes into account all of the perspectives and evidence you have gained. Note that you don't have to believe this new thought fully at the beginning, but just getting to this point will automatically weaken your problem worry, and your new thought will likely strengthen as you sit with it.

Column 7: Review and plan. To begin with, reread the original worry and review your mood about it in column 2. Now rerate your mood relative to the new thought that you have created and the evidence that you have collected. (In nearly all cases, you will notice a significant improvement.) Finally, make a plan for further action. If the issue is solvable, what are you going to do to overcome it? If it is floating, which technique are you going to use if it resurges?

We have put a thought record worksheet at the end of this chapter. You can also download a blank seven-column thought record, created by Carol Vivyan, from: http://www.get.gg/docs/ThoughtRecordSheet7.pdf.

Using Your Thought Records Well

As we have said, thought records are a useful technique to use on your journey toward the gold-standard technique of present contemplation. However, it is important to recognize that, if overused, they can actually become detrimental, as they appear to offer a level of control of thinking for those who already struggle with a desire for certainty. The worst outcome for someone using thought records would be to become obsessive or dependent upon using them every time a worrying thought arises, and being anxious about using them correctly.

This technique should be used selectively as a means to educate us about the types of worries we are having and the general overestimation of threats we are making. Thought records can improve our insight into the value of our thoughts and their impact on our mood. As a result, thought records can really help us familiarize ourselves with problem worry and reduce our anxiety to a level where we are more willing to see that in general our worries are poorly founded. This acceptance really helps us move on toward present contemplation.

Making New Appraisals

"Making new appraisals" is a useful technique that builds upon the thought record technique. It is a less controlled and rigorous version of thought records, and a further stepping-stone toward present contemplation. The important thing about the making-new-appraisals technique is that it operates in our thoughts, not on paper. And by responding to worried thoughts in general, the technique also encourages less certainty-seeking than thought records do.

Making new appraisals does not require you to seek evidence for or against your worried thought. Instead, it assumes that you are overestimating the significance of a worry thought and initiates a stream of secondary, more probable alternative thoughts. This leads to an internal narrative rather than a paper record, and it is helpful to know that this work broadens neurotransmission, working against narrow or certain thinking patterns.

Imagine non-worrier Dave. He steps out onto the disco

floor and begins to throw down some of his best moves. His friends smile and laugh, so he feels encouraged and becomes even more exuberant. At the end of the evening, he goes home feeling happy and confident.

Now imagine worrier Dave. He steps out onto the disco floor and begins his best moves. His friends smile and laugh, but he feels embarrassed and begins to worry that they are laughing at him. He walks off the dance floor and stands by the bar for the rest of the evening. He goes home feeling depressed and stupid.

Here's how the making-new-appraisals technique works: Imagine worrier Dave standing at the bar. His thought narrative might sound something like, "I'm sure they are all laughing at me because I was dancing weirdly. I am such a loser. . . . No, hold on a minute; maybe they were just laughing because they were happy to see me having fun. Maybe I was looking a bit funny for a moment there, but that's okay—if you turned the music off, everyone would look strange! I sometimes laugh when people are dancing, but it doesn't mean I want them to go away. They are all my friends, and I am sure they wouldn't have intended me to feel like this. I think perhaps I misjudged their reactions, although I still feel a little worried. Either way, I am going to go back and dance again!"

As you can see from Dave's revised appraisal above, he doesn't necessarily believe his new appraisal immediately. However, he does look at his predicament from different angles, producing alternative conclusions. Ultimately, this narrative stream leads him back onto the dance floor, and he ends up dancing the night away.

The making-new-appraisals technique can be used quickly and easily in any environment. However, just as with thought records, you must be wary that it does not become an unlimited stream of internal argument that seeks absolute certainty. The key to using this technique is recognizing that you may not believe your new appraisals very strongly—that is not important, but doing the exercise is. This technique should continue to build your insight, showing how often you overestimate the importance of worry thoughts. As the process undermines typical withdrawing or safety mechanisms, you should gain the confidence to know you can have occasional worry thoughts and get on with life anyway. In the next chapter we are going to introduce our gold-standard technique—present contemplation—but before we do so, we'll look at some things you should try to avoid.

Beware of Unhelpful Techniques

For those who have struggled with worry and intolerance of uncertainty for many years, it can be very tempting to turn to some less-than-constructive ways to reduce the pain. Here we have grouped them into two types: fairly unhelpful and very unhelpful.

1. *Fairly Unhelpful*

In our information age, we can easily believe that information is the answer to all problems. However, looking up stuff on the Internet will not only put you at risk of discovering some wrong answers but will also keep you on the "I-must-be-in-control" treadmill as you try to find out absolutely everything. If you do need to search the Internet for something, decide beforehand how much time you will devote to this and get someone to pull the plug when the time is up.

Spending time at the end of the day reviewing how things have gone can be a helpful reflective technique, and many people advocate keeping a journal. However, if you are a worrier, keep it to a few paragraphs a day max and limit the time you spend on it. Use a page-a-day diary and not a blank journal as your notebook. And consider writing it at the start of the day if journaling sets your mind racing last thing at night and potentially contributes to insomnia. (But if you must write at night, see Chapter 3, "What Happens When We Worry," for some advice on how to get to sleep afterward.)

Phoning a friend is a fine strategy on *Who Wants to Be a Millionaire?,* but people who worry can use this as a way of avoiding responsibility for decisions about uncertain things. The reassurance is short-lived, and it makes the worry worse in the long term. If this is you, then give this entire book to a friend so that he or she can be your coach and help you more in the long term.

2. *Very Unhelpful*

Getting totally drunk is one way to avoid the pain of life, but more often the problem is the more subtle use of alcohol: a glass to wind down or "just one before we go out to give me confidence." For a trial period, why not try sticking rigidly to one drink a day or even cutting out alcohol completely, especially when you feel stressed?

But alcohol is not the only addiction. Most of us are not into hard drugs, but do we use exercise, shopping, eating, self-harm, and so on in the same way as some people use alcohol? If you do so to a large degree, you may need to seek professional help before you tackle your worry.

Moving Out of the Comfort Zone

If you have ever watched *Survivor* or a similar show, you will have seen people taken well out of their comfort zone—and, often, really enjoying themselves. They sometimes ask themselves why they never did this type of thing sooner, and comment on how it has opened up a whole new world of opportunities.

Living a life of certainty sounds like a good and safe idea, but it is actually very restrictive. Imagine a world where every day you knew exactly what was going to happen, who you were going to meet, what they were going to say, and what food you would eat. If you suffer badly from worry, that might sound like heaven to you. So many people who worry avoid planning for the future for this very reason, claiming that they prefer to live day by day. However, to live such a life, you would need to live alone, meet a very small group of people, have repetitive conversations, and eat a pretty restricted diet. And you would also be at the mercy of the unexpected event, a visitor, a comment, or even a bug in your lettuce!

Uncertainty, on the other hand, broadens our horizons. Though it might be scary, there are opportunities for travel, for study in later life, for taking dance classes, for reconnecting with long-lost relatives, for cooking up a new dish—the list is endless. If you are reading this book, there are probably things about your life that you want to change.

Question: What are some things you would like to do if you were less of a worrier?

Answer: _____

_____

_____

Please note: You may not want to write anything here if it seems impossible right now and you don't want to be disappointed. But please do find a way to note your goals, even if they are only written on your heart as a secret between you and God.

Trying to Lose Control

The worry pendulum keeps on swinging relentlessly because people are trying to control something that cannot be controlled. A non-worrier would say that the obvious thing to do is to let go and stop trying to control it. However, most worriers are stuck with the desperate and determined belief that their attempt at control must be doing something, because if they weren't trying at all, then they would lose control completely, go mad, hurt someone they love, and possibly even die. . . .

So let's try to find out who is right, shall we? The worrier or the non-worrier? First consider this story:

> Rory got on the London train and sat down opposite a small man in a suit. As they left the station, the small man began tearing his newspaper into tiny pieces and throwing them out of the window. Rory pretended this wasn't happening, but after a while felt compelled to ask, "What on earth are you doing?" The small man replied, "It's very simple. I am keeping elephants off the track." "But there aren't any elephants on the track!" exclaimed Rory. The small man smiled. "It must be working then. . . ."

This rather silly story illustrates two points of view. To the small man, the act of throwing paper onto the track kept the elephants away and made the train safe. To Rory, the train was already safe because there were no elephants anywhere near the track—because this was the south of England! But who was right? The only way to find out was to stop throwing the paper out of the window—something the small man had never done because his protective belief and subsequent action were self-reinforcing.

Worriers have never tried to lose control. They have always tried to stay in control, and so far things have been fine. All right, worriers have felt anxious, lived with restrictions, and been unhappy—but the sky has not fallen on their heads, which they feared it would do if they stopped trying to be in control. Non-worriers know that being in such full control is not necessary, and is in any event impossible. They know that if the worrier were to stop worrying, everything would probably be okay, but who is right? The only way to find out is to stop trying to be in control—even to try to lose control. Stop throwing the paper out of the window.

Before you try to lose control, and we are going to ask you to try this in a few minutes, we need to put this in context and be clear what we are testing. We are trying to find out which of these two points of view is right:

- ◆ Worriers believe that, if they do not worry, they will lose control, the worry pendulum will swing wildly, something will go wrong, and they will have a panic attack.

◆ Non-worriers believe that everything will be fine because things can't be controlled by worrying, a panic attack is not the end of the world, and the thing feared probably won't happen anyway.

It's an Experiment

What we are talking about is an experiment, just like we used to do at school. However, this time, instead of finding out which things float when we put them in water, we are going to find out which of the above two statements is true. In the same way that we don't always know which things will float in water, we don't always know whether the worrier or the non-worrier is right. We may have a hunch, or know what we want to believe, but we really want to know.

We are asking you to do something, as this is how experiments work.

So, if you try to lose control and everything is still okay, this will help you disprove the first belief, and you will drive the pendulum less and be one step closer to the middle ground of uncertainty, one step closer to being a non-worrier. The other way to think about it is that you will be more able to listen to the non-worrying part of your brain, rather than being at the mercy of the worrier in you.

One small thing we need to mention: we can't promise that

things won't get out of control. There might be an earthquake or other freak event, in the same way that a rogue elephant that had escaped from London Zoo might stray onto the railway track. However, the probability of this happening is very small. But compare this with a 100 percent likelihood that the pendulum will keep on swinging if we don't attempt to change! The area in which you try to lose (or at least let go of) some control will depend upon what your individual worry themes are, whether they relate to work, safety, finances, or some other area. (You might want to read your notes at the end of Chapter 2 at this point.) Here are some things you can try. You should view them as mini-experiments, to find out whether the worrier in you is right or not. They are all fairly small steps at first. We are certainly not suggesting that your first experiment should be taking a round-the-world trip or climbing a mountain.

- Go for a local walk that you have never done before.

- Arrive slightly late for a social event/church.

- Allow (within limits) your children to choose what TV shows they watch.

- Ask your partner to pick a date type/location, and don't question it.

- Tell a close friend that you are reading this book.

◆ Let your grown-up child do the weekly grocery shopping.

◆ [Your idea . . .] _____

◆ [Your idea . . .] _____

Before you do one of these things, make some predictions (allowing your anxieties to express themselves) of what is likely to happen—for example, that you won't like it, that something will go wrong, that things will be unsafe. Write these down in the box below. When you have done the experiment, write down in the box what actually happened. Then do the experiment a couple more times and review again what happened.

Before: What did you predict would happen?
_____
_____
_____
_____

After: What actually happened?
_____
_____
_____
_____

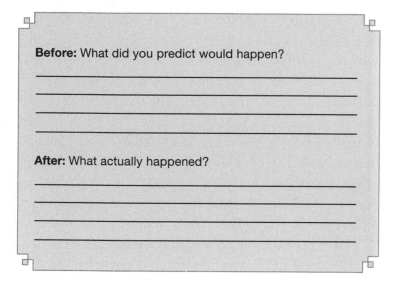

Before: What did you predict would happen?

_____

_____

_____

_____

After: What actually happened?

_____

_____

_____

The chances are that, when you try this, you will feel more anxious initially, but please keep on doing it. We think you will find that, first, no one has noticed you doing anything odd; second, you will feel better after a while; and third, breaking false rules is actually quite fun! You have moved from worry to laughing-at-worry, and that has to be a good thing. Please also note that no "sins" have been committed—not even by being a touch late for church!

Now do it again. And again, and again—until you are bored with doing it, or fed up with us for asking you to do it again and again. You get the point: really conquer it.

Tip: **Overthink**

Once you have mastered some of these things, it can be helpful to make sure that your anxious thoughts are really put to bed. A good way to do this is to go beyond the comfort zone and actively try to lose control or panic. For example, when out for your local walk, think as hard as you can of all the things that could go wrong—you could get lost, you could sprain an ankle or even break a leg, or you could lose your wallet. Sure, these things might happen (and we'll be praying that they won't!), but the aim is for you to learn that thinking these thoughts does not make these things happen.

It can also be helpful to write down these "worst-case scenarios" on a piece of paper. This is actually quite hard to do if you are a worrier, because most worriers believe to some degree that this will make them more likely to happen. Of course, they know this is not really possible, but the magical way of thinking seems to have got a hold over them. Tempting fate by writing them down, and seeing that nothing happens after all, is a good way to prove that the "magic" is not real. This is not putting God to the test; it is putting magical thinking to the test and finding it wanting.

Tip: **Get Angry**

Worrying thoughts will keep on coming, even if you do all the above. As we saw in Chapter 1, "Why We Worry," some people are more prone to worry because of their personalities, and these people, or those who have spent much of their lives worrying, are unlikely ever to be as relaxed as someone who has never really worried. So, at some point, they need to stop doing these exercises and take a different tack. Getting angry is one way to do this. The idea is to be angry with the worry and tell it off, instead of being angry with yourself or going along with the worry and treating it as a seemingly helpful thing.

Tip: **Postpone the Worry**

If a worrying thought pops into your head and you are in the middle of doing something else, then do not try to suppress it—it will only come back stronger later. However, what you can do is postpone the worry until later in the day. Say, "I'll worry about this later, because I am busy now." But you do have to keep the promise; otherwise your brain will quickly learn that this is an empty ruse.

When it comes to the time to worry, you will usually find that your heart isn't really in it and it is no longer a problem. This is not a perfect technique, but it can help with quite a lot of the worries that pop into your head. Some people even find it helpful to set aside a fixed half hour later in the day for having a good worry. You will need to work out how structured you need to be in postponing your worry.

Stop Trying Not to Worry

Let's move to the left-hand side of the pendulum, where people try not to worry. Trying not to do something, as we've seen, is not the way to get it out of your head. Yet worriers try all the time not to worry. They know worry is unhelpful, so they try not to do it. But this only works for a while.

Also, worriers aren't able to work out how much worry is appropriate, so they try not to worry at all. But then they worry about not worrying. It doesn't get them anywhere and keeps the problem going.

Exactly what you need to do instead will depend on your type of worry, and this is the subject of the next chapter. For now, we would just ask you to resolve to stop trying not to worry.

> Harriet was still a couple of weeks away from her ap-
> pointment with the orthopedic surgeon. To deal with
> her unhelpful approaches to worry, she did a number
> of things. She resolved to stop looking things up on the
> Internet and she asked her husband to organize a date
> night that week. She wrote a list of the scary words like
> "cancer" that had been going around in her head—and
> actually felt better as a result. She also confided her
> fears to a friend, who reassured her that it was quite
> normal to worry in such a situation, and they prayed

together. Whenever she found herself trying not to worry or trying to distract herself, she . . . (continued in the next chapter!)

To Wrap Up . . .

We have seen how simple techniques like thought records and making new appraisals can be used to challenge simple worries. But we have also seen how to start dealing with more complex and floating worries that do not respond to these two techniques. We have looked at both sides of the worry pendulum, and learned how to start losing control. We have also resolved to stop trying not to worry.

Exercises

Which do you do more: try not to panic or try not to worry? Are you someone who is typically aroused and stressed by worry, or do you shut down and do avoidant things?

_____

_____

_____

_____

Pick a common worrying thought that pops into your head, and try to challenge it using the thought record after the exercises.

_____

_____

_____

Note any new appraisals you think you might need to use regularly:

1. _____

2. _____

3. _____

Remind yourself of your worry themes from Chapter 2, "Understanding My Worry." Do you ever try to manage them in fairly unhelpful or very unhelpful ways?

1. My themes:

   a. _____

   b. _____

   c. _____

2. Fairly unhelpful: _____

3. Very unhelpful: _____

Write down what happened when you tried to put yourself outside your comfort zone.

1. What I did: _____

_____

_____

_____

2. What my predictions were: _____

_____

_____

_____

3. What actually happened: _____

_____

_____

_____

4. How I felt, having practiced this: _____

_____

_____

_____

Thought Record

Situation	Mood	Automatic thoughts/images (Main worry)	Evidence for main worry	Evidence against main worry	Alternative thoughts	Review and plan
Just left the house to meet a friend for a cuppa.	Slightly apprehensive 30/100	They won't like me. They have lots of friends but I don't. I don't have anything to talk about. It will not go well.	There have been times in the past when conversation has been difficult. We are at different life stages. I have not watched the news recently, so might not be up to date.	We have managed to have good times in the past anyway. Talking is not only my responsibility. Silence is OK occasionally.	There may be gaps in the conversation, but this is OK and they will pass.	Now 10/100 and feeling better. Floating worry with no solution. Commit not to worry about it and meet the friend.
Your worry here . . .						

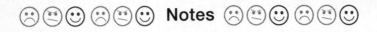 **Notes**

_____
_____
_____
_____
_____
_____
_____
_____
_____
_____
_____
_____
_____
_____
_____
_____
_____
_____
_____
_____
_____
_____
_____
_____
_____
_____
_____

7

Taking Action

Whatever you have learned or received
or heard from me, or seen in me—
put it into practice.
And the God of peace will be with you.

PHILIPPIANS 4:9

So far, we have looked at what worry is, how Christians relate to it, and how we deal quickly with simple worrying thoughts. In this chapter, we will learn how to deal with more ongoing worries. This will involve, as the verse above suggests, putting some things into practice and taking some actions. We will need to bear in mind the things we have learned so far, as our minds will easily slip into unhelpful ways of managing worry. However, with the right techniques, we pray that you will find that the "God of peace" is with you and that you can even experience his peace.

This chapter excites us, because we really do believe that recurrent worry is something that can be tackled rather than tolerated. In the "prison" letter to the Philippians, Saint Paul puts his mind-set and faith into practice, meaning that, while he is still scared at times, he is not worrying continually.

Two Ways to Peace

Remember our discussions on solvable worry and floating worry? (You might like to reread the end of Chapter 2 to remind yourselves of these.)

Solvable worry can be managed by taking action, actually doing something. Worrying is ineffective, but there are situations that can be influenced by what you do. For example, if you are worried about whether or not your pension is going to be big enough, you can see a financial adviser and act on what she recommends. The problem is that the worry paralyzes you and stops you from taking otherwise simple steps. So we are going to teach you about problem-solving as a way to take action with solvable worry.

On the other hand, floating worry, which is characterized by "what-if" thinking and worrying about worries, is not helped by any physical action you may take, because it is not about a solvable problem. Instead, we need to learn how to tolerate uncertainty—to stay in the midzone of the worry pendulum. We will teach you a different type of action to take, "present contemplation." But first let's talk about problem-solving.

Problem-Solving

In the 1980s, there was a program on children's TV called *Why Don't You?*—or, to give it its full title, *Why Don't You Just Switch Off Your Television Set and Go Out and Do Something Less Boring Instead?* Each week they would tell you about things to do rather than sit on the sofa—learn to ride a bike or visit a government office. Not many children actually did the things that were suggested, because they were firmly attached to the sofa by something called inertia. Inertia is the tendency to keep on doing what you have done for a long time. But problem-solving challenges inertia, and doing so overcomes your worry.

People who worry suffer from an inability to think clearly about what to actually do because of the fog of worry. Problem-solving is a structured approach to defining the problem that caused the worry in the first place, and uses options such as brainstorming, overcoming potential obstacles, and actually implementing the option chosen. You reflect afterward on what you have achieved and how your worry has disappeared. One of the unhelpful beliefs worriers can have is "At least I am doing something," and this is because worry takes energy, and it leaves you feeling drained. But of course worry itself is not problem-solving, because the problem is still there at the end. It just feels as if you have done something.

Because worriers typically worry rather than act, they may have accumulated problems that can actually be solved quite easily. They can come to believe that they alone have problems and that other people's lives are easy, or that they are somehow more prone to problems. Neither of these things is true. They may be out of practice at solving problems, but this can be remedied by experience

Seven Steps to Solving a Problem

To learn problem-solving, work through the boxes below. First, pick a manageable problem, such as not having sent a letter or always buying too much at the store. Over time, as practice improves your skills, you will be able to tackle even large problems, such as applying for a new job, using this technique.

Don't think too long about your answers: each section should take five minutes maximum. Also, try to be as specific as possible with your answers, because vague statements are more difficult to work with. You may like to do this with a friend at first, but over time we hope you will be able to do it by yourself. Remember that worriers can sometimes try to avoid taking responsibility for things by asking others to do them instead.

1. Identify the problem. Define it as clearly as possible.

_____

_____

_____

_____

2. Brainstorm as many solutions as possible. Rule nothing out, for now.

A _____

B _____

C _____

D _____

3. Look at the advantages and disadvantages of each solution.

Advantages	**Disadvantages**
A _____	A _____
B _____	B _____
C _____	C _____
D _____	D _____

4. Choose one of the solutions. List what you fear might happen.

Solution: _____

_____

Fears: _____

_____

5. Think of some practical steps you can take (but note that some risk will remain).

_____

_____

_____

_____

6. Carry out the chosen solution. What happened?

_____

_____

_____

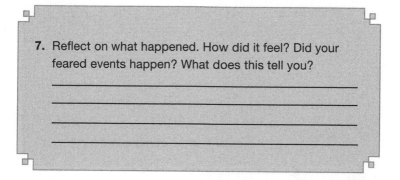

7. Reflect on what happened. How did it feel? Did your feared events happen? What does this tell you?

_____

_____

_____

_____

Even if things didn't go as well as planned, you can still learn something from what happened, such as what you might do differently next time. Problem-solving is a skill that you can apply to all worries about problems with potential solutions— it's just that you haven't gotten around to acting yet and have often worried instead. It will require practice, and you will improve over time, but it does work.

> Margo had been worrying for a while about what car insurance to buy. The information was all in an envelope on the dresser—it stared at her every time she went into the bedroom! One day she decided to try a problem-solving approach. She did an online brainstorm—a Google search—and noted down the first five suggestions. She made a simple list of the costs and main features of each policy, and picked one. She decided whether to pay up front or in installments,

asking her dad for advice on this. She bought a policy, and the whole process took half an hour. The documents arrived in the mail two days later. She felt so much better.

*Tip: **Ask once***

In the example above, Margo asked her dad for advice—exactly the right thing to do. However, if this is what you always do, or if you ask lots of people for advice and reassurance, then this can actually make the situation worse. It makes you dependent on others, and you never learn to work things out for yourself.

Also, remember that problem-solving is for immediate issues that are solvable by an action. If you use it as a technique for worry that is actually about a minuscule possibility or a situation where there is no solution, you will never learn to tolerate uncertainty. Seeking reassurance can become an obsessive-compulsive behavior that the worrier will resort to every time. If you catch yourself asking for advice regularly, resolve to stop doing this and follow the advice in the next section instead.

When There Is No Solution

Now let's look at the other type of worry, where there is no obvious solution: floating worry. Here the problem is the worry itself, rather than some underlying issue, such as debt or a deadline. We need to learn how to tolerate uncertainty.

The worry pendulum passes through a midzone characterized by uncertainty. Initially, being in the midzone will be unpleasant because it feels new and strange and will be accompanied by fairly high anxiety. However, worriers can learn how to tolerate this, and over time can spend increasing amounts of time in this zone. The anxiety will settle, and they will be able to relax. Things will still be uncertain, because that is the nature of some things, but this will be okay, and nothing bad will happen!

And now, let's finally get to the gold-standard technique we've been talking about: present contemplation, which is the ability to hold a thought (worry) in your mind and observe it, as if from a distance, without becoming too involved with it. We will also teach you about the common mistakes people make when trying to be contemplative, and how you can overcome them.

Present Contemplation

Present contemplation is the deliberate, patient focusing on something, holding it in your mind while not becoming consumed by its detail. Contemplation has been used by Christians throughout the ages, and it was made famous by the mystic theologians of the third to sixth centuries. Saint Athanasius described it as simply to "breathe Christ."

There is a biblical basis for this form of contemplation. Jesus made a repeated challenge to "keep watch," and there is a particular reference to a style of watchful awareness in Luke 12:35–48. Perhaps the verse that best identifies watchfulness as a mode of prayerful contemplation is Colossians 4:2, where Paul says, "Devote yourselves to prayer, being watchful and thankful." Watching and waiting for Jesus' return is a combination of action and reflection, of alert and attentive living in the present moment—not a time to be preoccupied with worrying.

Present contemplation is the opposite of being on automatic pilot, where you are able to do things with minimal conscious awareness. It is also very different from being over-involved and all in a state about something, as you are when you worry. In fact, the contemplation of the early Christian theologians was described as "the way of unknowing" or *via negativa*. It suggests that less information rather than more helps us find peace. Psychologists have described this as the "preconceptual." or the state before conscious thinking.

In present contemplation, you hold something in mind and spend time allowing yourself to interact fully with it. You observe it (in a sensing way, rather than thinking about it or analyzing it), describe it (and the associated emotions), and engage with it fully (not hiding anything). If you imagine floating worry as a trapdoor that the worrier continually falls through or avoids, present contemplation enables the worrier to examine the trapdoor without actually falling through it.

Present contemplation is our gold-standard technique in overcoming worry, because it trains the worrier to see their thoughts in a new way. It is like looking at them in a mirror, where you cannot reach out and grasp them—only observe them. It helps us to recognize that we are not our thoughts, nor the sum total of them. By changing the attitude of the worrier toward these thoughts to one of observation, acceptance, and distance, the thoughts lose the potency that creates a worry cycle. The repeated practice of present contemplation also trains the worrier to distinguish between the two types of worry, refocusing on those things worthy of genuine concern, rather than on thoughts that are insignificant or unrealistic.

To practice present contemplation, first pick a topic that is causing you some distress (typically one of the worry themes we looked at in Chapter 2, "Understanding My Worry").

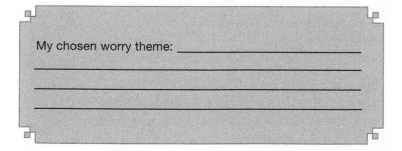

My chosen worry theme: _____

_____

_____

_____

Then pick a regular thought from within that theme. A good thought to choose is one that keeps popping into your head and causes you distress, so that you try to put it out of your mind.

My chosen distressing thought: _____

_____

_____

Note: *You might not be able to write it in this box if it is too distressing. This doesn't matter, as long as you are aware of a clear thought.*

Next, we want you to spend some time observing and considering this thought, bearing in mind the following concepts of contemplation. Do this without trying to avoid it or escape from it. You will find this challenging, because it is hard to do, and also new to you.

1. *Be nonjudgmental.* Even if the distressing thought is something you would normally regard as wrong or sinful, do not judge it or try to put it out of your mind, but allow it to stay. We are not asking you to condone a sinful thought or behavior, but rather to observe it for a while, as it may well be that your

quick judgment and dismissal of the thought and yourself are responsible for your ongoing depression or worry and the thought's recurrence.

2. *Be patient.* This refers not only to the fact that "getting" contemplation takes time (it's not a skill you will develop overnight), but it also refers to being patient and compassionate to yourself. Again, we are not asking you to put off dealing with issues indefinitely, but to realize that a quick-fix mentality may be part of the problem. Just as God is so very patient with us and deals with us tiny bit by tiny bit, we are aiming to take the same patient and compassionate approach toward ourselves. For a time, we want to see, yet not react.

3. *Be a beginner.* Little children are among the most able to enjoy the present, and often adults seem unable to do this, as they are filled with, and overly concerned with, thoughts about the past and future. Jesus encourages us to be like little children (Matthew 19:14), which means we may not understand everything that is going on, but we will experience so much more as a result.

4. *Be trusting.* Over time, we hope you will become more aware of what is going on in your body and

your mind and learn to trust the conclusions you come to. This is not putting your trust in man as opposed to God (Jeremiah 17:5), but learning to test what is going on and trust what you discern (1 Thessalonians 5:21).

5. *Be accepting.* We may have many things in our lives that we helpfully strive for, like being good parents or neighbors. But there are also many things we unhelpfully strive for, such as being thin, having perfect skin, or keeping up with the Joneses. Present contemplation challenges us to realize that it can be hard to tell the difference sometimes, and that God sees us and loves us just as we are. To accept who we are in his eyes is the first step toward growth, but for now we need to leave growth alone for a while and just accept things.

These concepts might be summed up in one phrase, "Be kind to yourself," or maybe in just one short word: "be." You could say that the thing we want you to "do" here is "be." There is a time and a place for a good kick up the backside, to be sure. However, we wonder if you are pretty good at doing that to yourself already, and we would ask you to consider how effective this has been in the past. Typically, people enter a cycle of self-directed thoughts, rumination on these, and a resulting low mood—which in turn makes the thoughts darker and the rumination even more like wading through treacle.

Maybe this is a good time to stop kicking and start being kind. We would suggest viewing contemplation as an alternative to rumination, so you can test whether or not what we say is true. Try ruminating, and we wish you all the best! Now try being contemplative, and see if that makes a difference. God's kindness to us is constant, merciful, enduring, even relentless, and he longs for us to follow his example. As the old saying goes, "How can we love our neighbors if we cannot love or accept ourselves?"

Things That Get in the Way of Present Contemplation

Worriers will do almost anything rather than tolerate uncertainty and be contemplative. We have already seen how people avoid the task at hand by doing something else (like housework), distraction (like buying a new CD), or doing things to stay in control (like crossing fingers or throwing bits of paper out of the window like Rory's fellow passenger in the last chapter). Present contemplation is no different, except that when you try to be contemplative, the things that spoil it are very subtle and seem like such a good idea at the time.

If you will permit us a slightly unpleasant illustration, imagine that you are trying to clean a toilet bowl that has some disagreeable marks on it and needs a good scrub. While it might be tempting to focus on the smell of the bleach, the fact that you will wash your hands really well afterward, the rhythm of the brush as it circles the bowl, and so on, at some stage you have to focus on the marks, i.e., get up close and scrub hard!

So, too, with these worrying thoughts. People often say things like, "I can't get thought X out of my mind," but we are going to show you that it actually would be more accurate to say, "I can't get thought X into my mind long enough to examine it, see it as untrue, and so get it out of my mind!" We need to be aware of the other, oh-so-valid thoughts that pop into our minds when we are trying to be contemplative.[1] We have listed some below, but you can probably add some of your own.

- ◆ Why is this happening to me?

- ◆ Am I doing this right?

- ◆ How long will this take—is this long enough?

- ◆ I'm finding this contemplative thing hard.

- ◆ I've really got the hang of this contemplative thing.

- ◆ Please, God, help me to focus on this thought.

A good question to ask might appear to be "How should we examine this thought?" However, this is actually not the right question to ask. We have found that when people practice being contemplative, they are actually less bothered by the thought and don't feel the need to examine it in that way. In any case, these are worries without answers, and being slightly uncertain about things turns out to be not as bad as you might think.

We started the story of Harriet (in Chapter 6) who had a lump on her shin. Let's finish the story now:

> . . . Whenever she found herself trying not to worry or distract herself, Harriet made herself aware of the present moment, of the many blessings she had and how she was enjoying so many things in her life right then. She also considered the word *cancer,* how it felt and what it sounded like to say it, and observed (without reacting) some of the thoughts that came into her consciousness as she spoke it aloud. These thoughts, as she observed them, actually just passed her by, and she realized they didn't have to be real or scary after all. There were many ways in which the meeting with the surgeon could go; but for now, what she could most helpfully do was enjoy the present.

One other reason that present contemplation is hard is that behind all the worry and anxiety often is a very deep and painful emotional core. It could be a fear that we will let someone down badly, or that we will make things much worse for everyone else if we don't stay in control. This emotional core drives us away from being contemplative and it keeps popping up its head.

We don't want to pretend that this technique is easy, but we do want to share with you that, in our experience, your fears do decrease in power over time if you use these techniques. Worry can be all about trying to stay in control, because deep inside you feel out of control. We want to take you to a place where inside you are more in control, even if on the outside you are more aware than before that you cannot actually control everything.

Present Contemplation and Christian Problems

Some Christians also struggle with the idea of present contemplation. They think it is dangerous and involves letting go too much, so that our own sinful nature, or even something (or someone) more sinful, might take control. People often quote 2 Corinthians 10:5 which says, "We take captive every thought to make it obedient to Christ," to suggest that we can never allow a thought to pass us by. To be sure, it is good for us to be aware of our thoughts and aim to make them more holy over time and in line with what Jesus would think, but this approach can result in guilt-inducing policing and micromanaging of our internal worlds, which is unlikely to be effective.

So perhaps a better phrase than "letting go" is "paying attention" or "living in the present moment." Matthew 6:34, Jesus' famous do-not-worry verse, which we looked at earlier, is actually translated in The Message Bible as *"Give your entire attention to what God is doing right now"* (emphasis added), intended as an alternative to trying to stay in control of the uncontrollable tomorrow. Psalm 118:24, as part of an otherwise under-siege psalm, says, *"This is the day the Lord has made; let us rejoice and be glad in it"* (emphasis added). Also, one of the greatest Christian books ever written, *The Practice of the Presence of God* by Brother Lawrence, is all about paying attention.

Present contemplation is choosing to remove from your mind the attempt to control the uncontrollable, and so has a sound psychological basis. Furthermore, if we believe in the indwelling nature of the Holy Spirit, then our contemplation can include the awareness of ourselves as we are in communion with God. Part of this is to consider ourselves in relation to God and the feelings this brings. It might be a good idea to start in a quiet place; but present contemplation, like many of the ideas in this book, is really a tool of discipleship and so to be taken on the journey. Being contemplative is no more restricted to kneeling in silence than worship is restricted to singing songs in church.

Some Christians struggle with the idea of letting a seemingly sinful or wrong thought exist in their minds without judging it. This seems to conflict with their morals or beliefs. For example, we looked at impure thoughts and subsequent worries about committing the "unforgivable sin." Because the thought is distressing, it is suppressed as soon as it pops into a person's head. However, as we know, suppressed thoughts tend to keep popping back into our minds until we can examine them by properly using techniques like present contemplation, and so will continue to cause us worry. To deal with them requires being nonjudgmental for a time, because judging leads to suppression of the thought and renders it inaccessible. What would you rather have, a few weeks of not judging a thought and so overcoming it, or a lifetime of suppressing a thought that just keeps on coming back?

Please note that we are not asking you to accept all thoughts uncritically or to use present contemplation as a way to decrease appropriate guilt. True guilt, as a result of an awareness of God's laws, has an important role in highlighting our need for salvation and making God's grace all the more sweet (Galatians 3:24). Its destination is the confession of sin and a sense of forgiveness, unlike the ongoing nagging doubt we are talking about here.

In all this, we are trying to remember that the goal is to manage the worry more helpfully, so that we might become more in touch with God and not feel the barrier of sins that we worry we have committed. We would suggest that using present contemplation in a nonjudgmental way is helpful in this context, and an appropriate technique for Christians. Ultimately, it will help the person grow deeper in faith and more sanctified as a result. All this to God's ultimate glory.

To Wrap Up . . .

We have looked at two different types of worry: worries with solutions (solvable worry), which can be addressed through good problem-solving, and worries that do not have solutions (floating worry), which can be addressed through present contemplation, allowing us to observe the worrying thoughts for long enough to address them. We have also examined some of the issues that present contemplation throws up for Christians.

Exercises

From the list below, decide which of these types of worry are solvable or floating. (Answers are in the Notes section at the back of the book.)[2]

1. Do I have enough gas in the car to make that journey?

2. If I were to move away, would I make any friends?

3. Am I exercising enough?

4. Have I committed an unforgivable sin?

5. Do I need to read through my essay again?

6. Does Sally really like me, or not?

7. Can I pay my gas bill this month?

Pick a worry in your life that is about a real event or a solvable problem, and work through the seven steps of problem-solving. Make some short notes here as well as in the boxes earlier in the chapter.

1. Problem: _____

_____

2. Chosen solution: _____

_____

3. Reflection: _____

_____

Practice present contemplation using the method outlined above.

1. What got in the way? _____

_____

2. How did you feel afterward? _____

_____

☹😕☺ ☹😕☺ **Notes** ☹😕☺ ☹😕☺

8

Worry and Hope

> We have this treasure in jars of clay
> to show that this all-surpassing power
> is from God and not from us.
> We are hard pressed on every side,
> but not crushed; perplexed,
> but not in despair . . .
> 2 CORINTHIANS 4:7–8

Congratulations, you've made it! To the end of the book, I mean. Reading books about how to overcome problem worry was often quite difficult for me (Will), because I would be concerned that I wouldn't "get it" or that I would find that the solutions just didn't work for me. Eventually, I realized that I couldn't be absolutely certain that it would help, so I decided I would do my best and trust that something would make a difference. When it comes to worry, it is often small, sometimes unnoticeable, shifts in attitude that have the greatest overall impact. Remember that a hairline crack in a glacier can shift a thousand tons of ice. Rob and I both hope that your worry has been thawed and fragmented through your experience of reading this book.

So How Do I Know I Am Better?

Better is not worry-free! The protective function of worry means that our brains have a radarlike element that scans for possible danger. In someone with problematic worry, that radar is way too sensitive. But we want to be clear that it is not our aim to turn it off altogether. We need to return it to a healthy level of sensitivity, so for the rest of your life you will continue to be interrupted by worrying thoughts. Sorry if this sounds like bad news, but actually that is how most people live and this is *better*.

The problem of the worrier is that these thoughts are very frequent and always acted upon. We have seen people recover from problematic worry and then, a few months later, call us in a panic because they are having some worrying thoughts. Typically, our advice has been to see these as normal and appropriate to whatever is going on at the time. The worrier often needs to do no more than, for example, shed some of the commitments he has taken on. I describe the knock-on impact of stress as sticky-thought syndrome. It is as if, during times of stress, negative or anxiety-provoking thoughts stick to our minds and are impossible to peel off. When we return to a relaxed state, the stickiness is gone, and we can brush off worrisome thoughts much more easily.

Keeping Perspective

After many years of battling with anxiety and worry, it is easy to lose perspective on how we are actually doing. This is true for all emotional issues; we lack objective opinions by keeping our problems private from others. We are also typically subjective when looking back at how we felt in the past. You feel what you feel when you feel it; canning it or keeping a sample for comparison later just isn't an option, unfortunately!

After years of personal work with fluctuating anxiety, I (Will) decided to take the plunge and book a consultation with an eminent psychiatrist, the author of a book I had found helpful. I had been worrying (as was typical) that perhaps I was missing a cure, or that I wasn't doing my CBT quite right. My consultation turned out to be a cure of a different kind! Having spent a very enjoyable hour chatting things through with the psychiatrist, this man leaned forward in his ostrich-skin shoes and told me what I already knew: that I had an anxiety disorder. Then he pleasantly congratulated me on everything I was doing and said, "You are an extremely functional and normal person, in fact, despite the existence of the disorder." I was "well" and had a normal level of worrying thoughts.

This might sound like an odd and personal thing to relay to you, but it is actually a commendation about this book. Despite struggling with objectivity about my worry, I am just one example of living proof that the tools and approaches we have outlined here actually work in practice. While I recognize that God may never grant me the absolute cure I pray for, he has granted me the cure that I need. I may never be worry-free, but I can certainly make healthy and godly decisions about how much to let worry interfere with my life and faith. "Well" is a state of being that I believe emanates first from the spirit. And when we make God the center of our approach to healing, "well" is never too far away.

Continuing the Journey

I (Rob) have found the idea of "life as a journey" really helpful. We travel from death to life, from ignorance of God to friendship with God, from worrying about the wrong things to worrying about the right things. This journey, like all other journeys, is unlikely to be a smooth slope upward, because that sort of thing happens only in the movies. It is far more likely to have ups and downs. Forrest Gump said, "Life is like a box of chocolates"— you never know what you're going to get; but unlike Forrest, we don't believe that life is quite so random and heartless. There will be tough times as well as good ones, for the thorns of this world do not affect us any less, just because we are Christians. Indeed, we follow a Savior whose journey led to the cross and crucifixion, so it would seem odd for us to wish for a stress-free life.

An Illustration from Motor Sports

In order to have continued success in our work with problem worry, it is essential that we carry our tool kit with us on the journey. Imagine setting off on the world-famous Paris–Dakar rally across the Sahara Desert without a spare wheel, extra oil, a shovel for the sand, and gallons of fuel and water. The reality is that the car will be fine on the tarmac roads of the Champs-Élysées, but it will have a few more problems on the scorching desert sand dunes!

1. Plan Your Route

Plan the route for your journey out of problem worry before you set off! We have shown you many different tips and techniques; you now need to choose how and when you are going to use them. Take time to make a rough plan for how you will respond next time you face a barrage of worrying thoughts. Making a plan means you are far less likely to switch automatically into old and unhelpful coping mechanisms.

Remember that you aren't responding to worry for the first time. You already have well-drilled and refined approaches to worry, despite these being unhelpful, and you must be intentional about choosing the new route you have planned when the moment comes.

2. *Keep an Eye on the Terrain*

Problem worriers can be so caught up with what is going on in their heads that they forget to look through the windshield of life at the terrain around them. The landscape of life will have a profound impact on the prevalence of worrying thoughts for two reasons. First, tough times by their very definition bring genuine concerns. Second, a stressed or exhausted limbic system produces higher volumes of irrational and intrusively frightening thoughts. If you are going through tough terrain at work, in relationships, or with your finances, you will need to anticipate even more worrying thoughts.

3. *Beware of Overheating*

Stress, as we have already seen, is a key factor in the battle against problem worry. Not only do stressful situations provide and provoke worries but stress itself diminishes our ability to deal well with them. When stressed, we often lose insight and feel tired or emotional. During these times, it can seem inevitable that we will end up ruminating on floating worries and that our moods will dip. If stress is high and worries are prolific, return to the plan and do what you can to create space and time in your life. Use present contemplation to bring your whole situation to mind with acceptance. Anticipate some discomfort as part of the journey at this time.

4. *Keep an Eye on the Dashboard*

So many of the worriers we know are highly gifted, capable, professional people with very full lives. Being a worrier has nothing to do with intelligence or motivation. Far from it, for it seems that some of the most intelligent and motivated people suffer from this problem. Part of the difficulty worriers have is that they are impossibly bad at self-care, so busy doing things or rushing, serving, or building that they never look at the dashboard to see if there are any red lights flashing.

Every engine is dependent upon oil, fuel, air, and the battery. The oil of the mind is a neurotransmitter called serotonin, and typically this depletes in times of high stress and exhaustion. Replenishment often comes in times of rest and contemplation. Fuel represents good food for the body and good spiritual nourishment for the soul. Air keeps the engine cool. We need clear air to gain perspective and clarity. When did you last take a vacation, for example? Finally, we need a fully charged battery. Are you charged up by God, fully plugged into him and the power of the Holy Spirit for your ongoing journey?

5. *Find a Driving Companion*

We want to ask you to share the journey, both with others and with God. I hate driving long distances alone. When I am tired, my wife notices and offers a snack, and we listen to music and tell each other stories. In the journey of life and the journey out of problem worry, we need companionship. The community of the church is a key part of your ongoing success in this journey, and we want to encourage you to get involved, be open and honest, and stay committed. If you do only one thing as a result of reading this book, make it sharing your worry problem with a trusted Christian friend and asking him or her to help you and pray for you.

6. *Are We Nearly There Yet . . . ?*

The story of the Bible is one of both "now" and "not yet." We see things like miracles and prophecies being fulfilled in real time, yet other prophecies and promises not being fulfilled immediately. Some, it seems, will never be fulfilled until heaven. However, we (as needy humans) want things to happen yesterday, especially when it means arriving at our desired destination. As kids, we used to annoy our parents by singing, "Are we nearly there yet?" over and over in the back of the car, just minutes into a long journey.

In John 17, Jesus prays for the future church, that they would be "one" (that is, united), but we know that this has not happened yet, despite lots of prayer by lots of people! So, too, with our worries. We believe that in heaven we will be free from many things that currently take up our brain space, including problem worry, but for now there will be challenges.

Ever since Genesis 3:17, we have been promised that life will at times be "toil" and pure hard work—and with that comes uncertainty . . . and worry. So we have to commit to persist with our journey out of problem worry in prayer and action for as long as it takes, which could well be longer than we would like!

Hold on to Hope

The curse of Genesis has always been accompanied by the hope of complete restoration. Hope can be difficult to hold on to when you are struggling with problem worry. Without a spiritual perspective, it can truly seem that there is no reason to hope. However, as Christians, we have a hope that stands firm beyond human reason: Jesus has risen from the dead, healings have happened and will happen, and more than a billion people believe, with us, that one day Jesus will come again in glory. In Romans 4:18, this is called "hope against hope" (cf. ESV).[1]

It is so important to hold hope for yourself and to have others around you who can hold hope for you while you journey out of problem worry. As a psychiatrist, I (Rob) often find myself doing this for people, saying, "I have seen this before, and I have seen people recover before." One word for the Holy Spirit is *Paraclete,* which means "alongside presence" and something in which we find great encouragement. On your journey from here, we pray that you will know the hope-filling alongside presence of the Holy Spirit.

Pray at All Times

We need to develop our general spiritual life, so that we are able to tap into prayer when we need to, rather than waiting for a worry crisis. As we've said before, if you had a bad back, a physiotherapist would ask you to do your exercises every day, rather than just before lifting a heavy box. So, too, we need to be strong in the muscles of our faith and in prayer, rather than waiting for times of more extreme need. Prayer at all times (Luke 18:1) means having an inner culture of prayer and God-consciousness, rather than praying occasionally for anything that springs to mind.

Present contemplation is a style of prayer where we can be kind to ourselves and nonjudgmental, while remembering God's love. It is important that our prayers around worry are based on contemplation and not on wanting everything to be taken away. We suspect you will have prayed the "get-me-out-of-here" prayer already and not received the answer you were hoping for. Therefore, we would suggest that to keep on praying for escape as your only prayer will lead to disillusionment or make your worry worse by causing the pendulum to swing wildly.

Remember that God's divine action in releasing a miraculous healing is always possible when you are open to him. He will do his work, but for now we encourage you to use contemplative prayer (present contemplation) as your model. Contemplation allows us to rest in Christ and our relationship with him, while tolerating unanswered questions. It encourages our patience and trusts in God's goodness, without demanding immediate change.

Conclusion

Search me, O God, and know my heart;
test me and know my anxious thoughts.
See if there is any offensive way in me,
and lead me in the way everlasting.
—PSALM 139:23–24

This book has been a journeyman's guide to worry, the type of anxiety that grumbles and groans in the background, causing rumination. It breeds even more uncertainty than it tries to overcome. We have led you on this journey from understanding worry and how the brain processes it, to learning some essential techniques for moving on. We have encouraged you to live in the tension between knowing that hope exists and seeing the fruit of that hope.

We have also been clear that worry has a healthy protective function, and that to some degree uncertainty will always be our companion this side of heaven. We know that, for many worriers, the internal world is only part of the problem: their contexts, family lives, work pressures, and personal situations all contribute to the pain and uncertainty of life, and hence there are both solvable and floating worries at play.

Psalm 139 is most often used as an encouragement that God knows us even from our mother's womb (verses 13–16), but it also covers the whole span and spectrum of human existence. It ends with verse 23 about anxieties and verse 24 about sin. These two frailties of sin and suffering are the two most profound markers of the human state. We all sin, and we all suffer or struggle with something—these are the results of being born. They are distinct, in that to suffer with worry is not a sin; yet they are the same, in that the hope of relief comes from being born again, born of God, and adopted into his family.

They are also the same in that God, the Father of this new birth, takes an interest in them both. The psalmist invites God into his internal world, knowing that his sins are forgiven and that there is hope for all who worry and are anxious. His goal is the transformation of his heart, an ongoing task for all who love and follow God. Whatever we learn on the way, nothing is more transforming than knowing that we are his children and he is our Father. Our identity in the Prince of Peace is the best assurance of a victory over worry. I know who I am because I know whose I am (see 2 Timothy 2:12).

Your journey has begun, and we hold hope as you take courage and apply what you have learned here to life. Your journey and ours will be ongoing, but be encouraged, for this is a path that many have walked before, and our hope is real. We are privileged to have had this opportunity to share the road with you and wish you every blessing in Christ as you continue to find freedom and joy in Jesus.

Exercises

Look back at the motor sports example:

1. What is your plan/map for the way forward?

_____

_____

2. What do you recognize as areas of strength/weakness for the journey?

_____

_____

3. What resources/preparations would ensure that the journey is as smooth as possible?

_____

_____

What are your goals after reading this book?

1. Look back at the exercises in Chapter 1, "Why We Worry," to see what you wrote about your goals. Have they changed?

_____

_____

2. What do you think of the idea of living a fulfilled life while still struggling with worry to some degree? Is this possible or not? Discuss this with a friend.

_____

_____

3. Read Will van der Hart's "Driftwood" contemplation in Appendix 2. What does the word *hope* mean for you?

_____

_____

4. What are your human hopes? It is okay to have some!

_____

_____

5. What are your hopes against hope?

_____

_____

6. What are your eternal hopes?

_____

_____

Think about your prayer life. What is the balance between get-me-out-of-here prayers and contemplative prayers? What can you do to change or redress this balance, if necessary?

_____

_____

_____

_____

Visit www.mindandsoul.info/worry and have a look at what is available. Don't forget to register for more material.

Having finished this book, what is the one thing you need to do next?

My next task is: _____

_____

I will do this on: _____

_____

☹ 😑 ☺ ☹ 😑 ☺ **Notes** ☹ 😑 ☺ ☹ 😑 ☺

Appendix 1

Going Deeper

The next few pages contain material that will enable you go deeper in some areas. This is not essential for most journeys out of worry, but may answer some questions you have had along the way, and direct those of you who need it to more resources and help.

What to Do When Worry Really Takes Hold

Self-help books like this one are useful, especially if you read them with a friend or relative who can help you think through the issues and stay on track. However, they are the first level of intervention. There will be some people who need more help with their worry—and this might include any or all of the following: seeing your doctor, seeing a therapist (preferably a CBT therapist), seeing a psychiatrist, and taking medication. It is unlikely that worry pure and simple would result in you needing to go into the hospital, but sometimes ensuing depression can be so severe that this becomes advisable.

Because all this sounds a bit scary, this section contains

resources to help you find the right person to talk to.

Remember, all of the people in these jobs do them because they want to help those with mental-health problems and may even have had such problems themselves. However, if you are wary about seeing someone, it is absolutely fine to take someone along for the consultation and explain that you would like that person to sit in, at least at the beginning. As a psychiatrist, I (Rob) know how grateful I am when people bring someone along to the consultation, as it lets me know the person has support and also that together they are more likely to remember the conversation!

Seeing a Therapist

If this book really resonates with you and you think you need more help, we would recommend that you see your general practitioner and ask to be referred on. We would also say that you are better off seeing a secular therapist who is good, than a Christian therapist who is not so good. Hopefully, you can find a good Christian therapist, although sometimes it is helpful to see someone who does not share your faith, as you really have to examine many of your assumptions that may have unwittingly been keeping the problems going.

We would recommend seeing a cognitive-behavioral therapist if you have ongoing and chronic worry. A number of other types of therapy offer some help in this area, including person-centered therapy and psychodynamic therapy. However, it is CBT that has the most evidence of effectiveness with worry and forms the basis for this book. The national association of accredited CBT therapists, all of whom have trained to postgraduate diploma level, is the National Association of Cognitive-Behavioral Therapists. You can find out more at nacbt.org.

Getting Urgent Help

There are times when you need to talk to someone immediately, and the list below gives you the relevant telephone numbers.

Your local Emergency Room: These are open twenty-four hours a day, and you can just walk in.

Call 911: In a life-threatening emergency, when you cannot get to the hospital, you can call 911 free from any phone, including pay phones and mobiles, and ask for an *ambulance.*

The Samaritans: A confidential phone line you can call if you are feeling suicidal: 1-800-273-talk; www.samaritansusa.org.

What to Do If You Start Slipping Backward

Over the next few months, we hope that you will continue to grow more and more in managing worries and enjoying life. However, as you are aware already, this journey is unlikely to be totally smooth. There will be some bumps along the way.

How we react when a setback comes along can make all the difference. If we are able to roll with the punches a bit, this can mean that we ride over the setbacks. If, however, we panic and overreact, predicting that this will result in disaster, a small setback can indeed turn into a larger disaster, and we can end up back at square one.

The following list is something you should read if you are having a bumpy ride. We hope it will keep your thinking on track, and mean that the bump will only be a bump and not a disaster. Take the time to make some notes about what you feel about each tip.

Practical Tip	Your Notes
1. You know that setbacks are likely to occur. What happened was always likely to happen at some point.	
2. Setbacks are temporary and short-term hiccups and will usually settle after a few days.	

Practical Tip	Your Notes
3. Setbacks are not themselves disasters and do not mean that you are back to square one.	
4. A setback can be a positive experience, allowing you to build on the skills you have learned.	
5. Setbacks can be predicted. Identify some situations where they might occur.	
6. Do not avoid whatever caused the setback—this needs to be dealt with.	
7. Do not escape from the situation by leaving it or drinking alcohol—it *will* settle.	
8. You have learned a range of skills in this book. Use them now, or read through your notes.	
9. Set yourself targets to get back on track. Start off with some short-term ones to get you to tomorrow.	
10. If you have tried all of these, talk to someone who will be able to give you good advice. Who will you talk to?	

Keep a note here of situations where you might likely to have a setback:

_____

_____

_____

Keep a note here of what you did when you experienced a setback, and what happened:

_____

_____

_____

What About More Severe Anxiety?

Panic Attacks

These are extreme spikes of anxiety, often caused by a trigger, such as heights or spiders. Fears like this are quite common and can be very limiting: for example, someone never going on a plane to see a loved one overseas. In between attacks, many people are fine and have no anxiety, although quite a few people have background worry (and that is where this book is helpful).

A good CBT therapist should be able to help you with a simple panic or phobia in just a handful of sessions, so it is well worth getting your general practitioner to refer you for a short course (or you can find a CBT therapist at nacbt.org).

More About Generalized Anxiety Disorder (GAD)

Psychiatrists use sets of symptoms to diagnose mental illnesses, as the problems are not those for which there can be blood tests or X-rays. A common list of GAD symptoms (in brief in Chapter 3) comes from the *Diagnostic and Statistical Manual of Mental Disorders,* commonly called *DSM-IV.*[1] You shouldn't worry too much about whether you can tick off all the items on this list, but instead ask yourself, "Does this describe me fairly well?" There are fact sheets on GAD that can tell you more, or which you can give to friends, employers, and relatives to explain what is going on.[2]

On the Internet, you will easily find copies of something called the Penn State Worry Questionnaire (PSWQ).[3] A score of more than 57 is generally thought to reflect significant GAD. The maximum score is 80, and people who score close to this will have more severe worry problems than this book will be able to help them with; in such cases we would advise you to see your doctor as soon as possible. Over time, significant worry really can eat away at you and affect every aspect of your life—your weight and mood, for example—and can turn into significant depression.

PSWQ score	Less than 57	More than 57	More than 65	More than 70
Severity of GAD	Mild GAD or part of the normal range of personality. You have a tendency to worry and analyze, but you can live alongside it.	Moderate GAD, where your worry is beyond just annoying and at times affects how you function.	Severe GAD, where your worry is nearly always a problem and often affects your functioning.	Very severe GAD, where your worry is very severe, significantly handicaps you, and probably also causes depression.
How to use this book	This book may explain some of your feelings and help you to understand some Bible passages you have found hard until now.	This book is really designed for people like you to work through, and should make a major difference to how you think and feel.	This book will be helpful, but you will need some help—maybe from a friend or relative who can read it with you, or possibly from a professional via your GP.	This book will not help all that much with your worry, and you will need professional help, but it may help you understand some things and how your faith fits in.

Other Complex Anxieties

Worry (or GAD) is one of a number of complex anxiety disorders, of which three others are mentioned briefly below. The main difference between a complex anxiety disorder and milder or shorter-lived problems is that the former has really got its teeth into you in a way that means you will be unlikely to get better without the help of a specialist. However, good CBT really can make a difference, so please do seek help. A psychiatrist also offers medication sometimes.

OCD (obsessive-compulsive disorder) means intrusive (obsessive) thoughts, feelings, or images about things that sufferers then feel compelled to neutralize by an action. Often the obsessions are about such things as hygiene or orderliness, but these are on top of deeper fears about being powerful and out of control, or harm coming to a loved one. The compulsions are partly about restoring hygiene or orderliness, but also about controlling the power or protecting the loved one. Treatment involves accepting intrusions (we all have them), resisting compulsions, and bearing the deeper fears. Some people's compulsions can be internal thought processes (such as counting in a particular way); this internal type of OCD has many similarities to GAD.

PTSD (post-traumatic stress disorder) is where the sufferer experiences flashbacks or nightmares of a past trauma, as though it were still happening. He or she is physiologically aroused, as if it is about to happen all over again and, therefore, avoids similar situations. People may never have had any mental health problems before the trauma, so may also become quite depressed, wondering why this is happening to them and why they can't manage it. People can also assume that, because something bad has happened to them, they must have done something wrong. Treatment involves correcting the processing of the memory and challenging the avoidance.

Bulimia nervosa (and to a certain extent other eating disorders, too) is a cycle of anxiety about weight or a current life issue, followed by relief through bingeing and purging. Anxiety cycles are self-maintaining, because when you are anxious, there is nothing you would rather do than seek relief—yet the relief is only temporary. If you are sick more than three times a day or losing weight, you should seek medical help.

What Is the Cognitive-Behavioral Approach?

Cognitive-behavioral therapy, or CBT, was first clearly described by an American psychiatrist and psychoanalyst named Aaron T. Beck. As a psychoanalyst, he spent a lot of his time trying to interpret and discover his patient's unconscious beliefs and anxieties. However, one day it occurred to him that it might be easier actually to ask people what conscious thoughts were in their heads. This is not to say that psychoanalysis is no good—it is very good for some types of problems—but for many common mental health problems, CBT has been found to be the most effective form of therapy and the one most often recommended by the NHS. At its core are questions about thoughts: What went through your mind? What did you think next? How does this thought relate to this other thought? And so on. CBT never asks the why question, although you often end up realizing why yourself!

As well as thoughts, CBT looks at behaviors, especially avoidant behaviors and times when you have escaped from a situation. CBT therapists are also interested in the more subtle safety behaviors that allow you to keep on going in an anxious situation, but which never fully help—and actually make the problem worse in the long term.

The idea is that, by changing unhelpful thoughts and modifying unhelpful and cyclical behaviors, you will be able to help your mood. This typically takes around twelve sessions—two or three for helping you to understand your problem, two or three to get more evidence about how to change, three to six for changing, and two or three for making sure things are really fixed and that you know what you need to keep on doing in the future. Some simple phobias will be quicker, but some more complex anxieties and ruminations can take up to thirty sessions. The sessions are typically weekly or biweekly and about an hour long.

A number of websites teach CBT skills online, such as www .llttf.com [Scottish] and www.moodgym.com.au [Australian]. These two are freely available to all Internet users and are backed up by good scientific data.

Prayers and Contemplations for Times of Anxiety

These prayers will be helpful as you work through this book. It is only with God's strength that we are able to make this journey. Rest on him and walk with him as you go. You may also find Psalm 23 helpful.

Dear Lord,
You were in the boat when the disciples were afraid at the height of the storm. At this moment, I feel deeply afraid and adrift on a sea of worries. I know that you are with me, even when you seem far away. Help me, Father. Come close to me and calm the wind and the waves. I trust in you, despite what my senses are saying to me. I am clinging on to the truth of your promise never to leave me or forsake me. In Jesus' name, Amen.

Jesus,

You faced the greatest of fears in the Garden of Gethsemane. I am facing a great fear in my life at this time, and I need your grace to stop me from running away. I pray that you would be my comfort and guide through these difficult times. Reaffirm in me that you work for the good of those who love and fear you. I know that, with your presence, I can journey through this thing that I fear. I pray that on this journey you would cause me to grow in faith and trust. In your precious name, Amen.

Dear Lord,

I find it so easy to condemn myself in this struggle against worry. I always seem to feel that I have been weak or faithless. I pray that you would release me from these guilty feelings and lead me forward with courage. I trust in the healing work you are doing in my life. I know that every difficult moment is a new opportunity to put these tools into practice. Bless me, Jesus, with the diligence to do the work that you have set before me. I know that you delight in my obedience, and I choose to step forward on the road of change today. In your name, Amen.

Dear Lord,

John 14:25–27 says: All this I have spoken while still with you. But the Counselor, the Holy Spirit, whom the Father will send in my name, will teach you all things and will remind you of everything I have said to you. Peace I leave with you; my peace I give you. I do not give to you as the world gives. Do not let your hearts be troubled and do not be afraid. Amen.

Jesus,

Today I choose your peace in the face of turmoil. I choose trust in the presence of doubt. I choose courage when my will feels weak. Today I have decided to be kind to myself when it is my tendency to be critical. Today I will rest in your presence when I might try too hard. I will be a dispassionate watcher when I feel tempted to overanalyze my thoughts. Today I will be obedient to your call when I might run like Jonah. I will make light of what might have been heavy. Today I can do all this only through Christ who strengthens me. So I pray, Lord Jesus, for your strength and power in all of this and more. For your glory, Amen.

Dear Lord,

Job 28:11 says that you "search the sources of the rivers and bring hidden things to light." I open my heart and mind to you, and pray that you might search me and bring to light both the general themes of my worries and the deeper sensitivities and hurts that have kept them alive. I long to have a mind that is free to praise you and hands that are liberated to do your will. I am tired of my preoccupations, and disheartened at my inability to trust and obey. I ask you for the courage to stand and face what has made me afraid, and pray that as you bring these things into the light, they may be disempowered and overcome. Amen[1]

Driftwood

I was once part of the vine,

Created in God's image and unified with him,

Fruitful, purposeful, pure.

I was broken off by sin, mine and others.

I damaged myself and was damaged;

I oscillated away from the life of the vine and was consumed by
the sea.

My identity was corroded by the salty waters;

I was tumbled in the waves and dragged through the shingle.

I became trapped in the ebbs and flows of the tide.

I realized that I was but helpless driftwood,

Unable to save myself, unable to undo what had been done,

Muted in emotion, broken in my body and crushed in spirit.

I have been picked up, gently collected from the shore, plucked
from the water's edge.

The hand that made me holds me once again.

I am loved.

I am being restored; the scars of the sea have become places of
beauty.

They speak of the character of my Savior,

As if the distance to my soul is thinner there.

I am not alone.

The vine of my history is the vine of my future.

I belong again, fruitful, rooted, and secure.

My journey of healing will one day be complete,

But for now I hope in the promises of the One who picked me
  up from the shore,
The One who brought me home.

by Will van der Hart

Other Resources

Christian Resources

Chris Williams, Paul Richards, and Ingrid Whitton, *I'm Not Supposed to Feel Like This: A Christian Approach to Depression and Anxiety* (London: Hodder & Stoughton, 2002), www.fiveareas.com.	The classic Christian book on anxiety and depression from a CBT point of view. Easy-to-use techniques, supported by relevant Christian illustrations. More about depression than worry, but still very relevant.
Edward T. Welch, *Running Scared: Fear, Worry & the God of Rest* (Greensboro, NC: New Growth Press, 2007), www.ccef.org.	From the biblical counseling organization Christian Counseling & Educational Foundation (CCEF), Ed Welch brings an informed perspective to why we worry and how God speaks directly to the underlying fears.

Other Resources for Worry

Chris Williams, *The Worry Box: All You Need to End Anxiety* (Five Areas, 2009), www.fiveareas.com.	Four little books in a box: *Understand Anxiety, Face It, Fix It, Forget It*. And even the box helps you stop worrying. A simple and fun way to deal with panic, anxiety, and worry.
Kevin Meares and Mark Freeston, *Overcoming Worry: A Self-Help Guide to Using Cognitive Behavioural Techniques* (London: Robinson, 2008), www.overcoming.co.uk.	Part of the well-regarded Overcoming series, this book looks at how worry is the issue, not the things you worry about. With detailed self-help information and lots of tools to help you change, this is a hard-work, self-help book that will really make a difference.
Michel Dugas and Melisa Robichaud, *Cognitive Behavioural Treatment for Generalized Anxiety Disorder: From Science to Practice* (Oxford, UK: Routledge, 2006).	A heavyweight theoretical and scientific background to generalized anxiety disorder, including much of the evidence for the CBT models on which we base this book.

More Help Online

The Mind and Soul website is a British resource that has a huge amount of information about emotions and faith and how they relate. We have created a special section to accompany this book at www.mindandsoul.info/worry, where you can share with other readers, ask questions, and read far more about worry that we could ever put in a book.

Join Other Readers Online

You can read this book with others by joining our online forums and chat, as well as access additional material on anxiety and worry by visiting: www.mindandsoul.info/worry.

To help you get the most out of the book, you will find the following:

- ◆ forums for each chapter

- ◆ rating scales for you to download to monitor your progress

- ◆ talks on worry to listen to

- ◆ all the other resources of the wider Mind and Soul website

Glossary

Antidepressants: General practitioners and psychiatrists may offer medication to assist with severe worry that meets the criteria diagnosed as generalized anxiety disorder. These will typically be modern antidepressants. These will be at higher doses and for longer periods than medications for depression. A psychiatrist may offer other types of medication, such as pregabilin (Lyrica), but this should only be under specialist supervision and after talking treatments have been tried.

Cognitive avoidance: When an internal, thought-based activity takes the place of thinking about something that is more challenging, and thereby prevents the person from learning.

Cognitive-behavioral therapy (CBT): A type of talking therapy, where thoughts and behaviors are made more helpful with the aim of helping the person's mood. Typically in worry, this involves addressing anxious thoughts and worry rules and avoidant behaviors, with the aim of making the person less anxious and less prone to worry.

Complex anxiety disorders: Disorders such as worry, post-traumatic stress disorder, obsessive-compulsive disorder, and some eating disorders, where things have been going on for so long and are sufficiently complex for the problem to be likely to be self-maintaining, even if the original trigger is removed. This is often characterized by a background anxiety between acutely anxious episodes.

Depression: A pervasive feeling of unhappiness and low mood that lasts for two weeks or longer. Doctors make the additional distinction of *clinical depression* where there are also symptoms in the body, such as weight loss, poor concentration, and disturbed sleep or libido.

Floating worry: This is worry about things where there is no answer to be found, no matter how much you worry. Present contemplation is the recommended technique.

Generalized anxiety disorder (GAD): A severe form of worry, accompanied by bodily symptoms, such as restlessness, fatigue, difficulty in concentrating, irritability, muscular tension, and sleep disturbance.

Medication: See Antidepressants.

Panic: A more short-lived anxiety attack, typically in response to an external trigger (such as a spider or heights) or an internal trigger (such as chest pain or palpitations, which can be quite normal but interpreted as catastrophic). The person is typically fine between attacks, although significant worry can develop if the problem is not addressed correctly or they seek lots of reassurance as opposed to understanding.

Pendulum: See Worry pendulum.

Personality: A deep-seated and relatively permanent aspect of a person's overall character and presentation to others. Often rooted in genetic contribution or early-life experience. Personality traits and disorders are amenable to treatment over a long period of time, but the underlying personality will remain. Psychologists define five main aspects to personality: openness, conscientiousness, extraversion, agreeableness, and neuroticism.

Present contemplation: The practice of observing a thought or emotion in a nonjudgmental, patient, trusting, and childlike way, thus enabling the emotion to be processed in a more objective manner.

Problem-solving: A stepped approach to breaking down problems and solutions into manageable chunks, to help you make sense of what is happening and actually see some results.

Safety behaviors: Activities undertaken instead of feared activities that make the person feel slightly better in the short term, but ultimately prevent him or her from learning things that will decrease worry. Sometimes safety behaviors are extreme, such as escaping from a situation or avoiding it entirely. More often they are more subtle, and the person manages to "struggle on through" anxious times. However, he/she is prevented from learning new ideas.

Solvable worry: This is worry about things that do actually have a solution, and where action can be taken either immediately or in the near future. Problem-solving is the recommended technique.

Uncertainty: The condition of not being 100 percent sure what is going to happen next and, for worriers, the resulting anxiety. However, over time, a person can learn techniques to tolerate uncertainty. Faith is also important here.

Worry pendulum: The worry pendulum is an analogy we use to describe what is going on in the mind of a worrier. It swings between trying not to worry (something the worrier cannot sustain as he/she has too many positive beliefs or worry rules about worrying), and worrying too much (which is unpleasant and might result in the worrier losing control or having a panic attack). Worriers avoid the middle ground of uncertainty, which is at the center of the pendulum's swing. However, this is where they need to spend time in order to manage worry more effectively.

Worry rule: A strongly held belief about the role of worry. Most worriers have more positive than negative beliefs about worry, and so continue to worry even when it is not of benefit. Beliefs such as worry rules can be examined, reappraised, and changed in just the same way as thoughts can, although there is typically more emotion involved, and consequently change is often slower.

Worry theme: A major and recurring focus of worry, typically covering a number of individual worries. Most people have one or two themes. Knowing your worry theme is important in being able to label intrusive worrying thoughts for what they are.

Worry: The ongoing thinking over and over of things, with the aim of finding an answer. The worrier is less obviously anxious than people who have panic attacks, but can be more disabled.

Notes

Introduction

Guidance produced by the National Institute for Health and Clinical Excellence is available from www.nice.org.uk/CG022 and recommends cognitive-behavioral therapy—the approach used in this book.

1. Why We Worry

1. The Myers Briggs Type Indicator (MTBI) is one of a wide range of personality tests. It is common, seems easy to use, and tends to give people (of a certain personality type) a "Wow, how did they know that about me?" experience. In the right hands, it can be a useful tool, but it is not psychologically robust and tends to minimize the neuroticism dimension of normal healthy personality.

2. This illustration is taken from Meares and Freeston, *Overcoming Worry* (more details in Appendix 3) and is used with permission. You can read a much longer version on page 5 of that book.

3. **What Happens When We Worry**

1. If this is something that seems to describe you very well and you would like to know more, then you can read the work done by Professor Adrian Wells and his colleagues at the University of Manchester. Details of his research and publications can be found at www.psych-sci.manchester.ac. uk/staff/ AdrianWells.

4. **Worry Fuel: What Keeps My Worries Alive**

1. If you suffer from depression as well as GAD, you will need to work out which one to tackle first. The basic rule is the one that came first. If your GAD over time causes you to live a restricted life and you have become depressed, tackle the GAD first. A psychiatrist or psychologist can help you with making this choice.

2. OCD Action is the leading UK charity helping people with obsessive-compulsive disorder, which has a lot of similarities with problematic worry (visit www.ocdaction.org.uk).

3. D. W. Holowka, M. J. Dugas, K. Francis, N. Laugesen, "Measuring Beliefs About Worry: A Psychometric Evaluation of the Why Worry II Questionnaire." Poster presented at the Annual Convention of the Association for the Advancement of Behavior Therapy, New Orleans, 2006.

5. **My Faith and My Worry**

1. D. Martyn Lloyd-Jones, *Studies in the Sermon on the Mount* (Leicester: Inter-Varsity Press, 1959).

6. **Tolerating Uncertainty**

1. Christine A. Padesky and Dennis Greenberger, *Mind Over Mood: Change How You Feel by Changing the Way You Think* (New York: Guilford Press, 1995).

7. **Taking Action**

1. The technical name for this is "cognitive avoidance," and it is like any other kind of avoidance, just less obvious, and more difficult to challenge.

2. 1=S, 2=F, 3=S, 4=F, 5=F, 6=F, 7=S.

8. **Worry and Hope**

1. The English Standard Version is says in Romans 4v18, "In hope he [Abraham] believed against hope, that he should become the father of many nations," but other translations capture the essence as well—hope that goes beyond what "human hopes" would lead you to expect or trust in.

Appendix 1: **Going Deeper**

1. The full reference is the *Diagnostic and Statistical Manual of Mental Disorders, Version IV,* published by the American Psy-

chiatric Association in 1994. The alternative is the *International Classification of Diseases, Version 10,* published by the World Health Organization in 1990. *DSM-V* will be coming out in May 2013, and it is thought that it will place less emphasis on the physical/bodily symptoms of worry, retaining only restlessness and muscular tension, because these are felt to be most specific to GAD, as opposed to other anxiety disorders. You can see more at www.dsm5.org

2. A large number of leaflets can be found on the website of the Center for Clinical Investigations in Western Australia: www. cci.health.wa.gov.au (select Resources > For Consumers > Info Pax called "What? Me Worry!?!"). This questionnaire is the main one used by psychologists to measure the severity of people's worry.

3. You can read more about its development and accuracy in this scientific paper: T. J. Meyer, M. L. Miller, R. L. Metzger, T. D. Borkovec, "Development and Validation of the Penn State Worry Questionnaire," *Behaviour Research and Therapy* 28 no. 6 (1990): 487–495.

Appendix 2: Prayers and Contemplations for Times of Anxiety

1. Jonathan Aitken, *Prayers for People Under Pressure* (New York: Continuum International Publishing, 2004). Used with permission of the author.

In *The End of Worry: Why We Worry and How to Stop,* Will van der Hart and Rob Waller expose the reasons behind our worry, why we love to worry, and how to overcome it. Worry is a process—and as we actually follow through on the process and become comfortable with uncertainty, we can learn to live with a healthy level of worry. No longer do worriers have to struggle to just get over it, trust God, read the Bible more, or have more faith. Will and Rob offer solid, proven techniques to eliminate guilt and embrace risk, and not let worry have the last say.

Discussion Questions

1. The authors present the typical Christian's dilemma as between being consumed by worry and ashamed about a lack of faith and trust in God. How does this compare to your experience with worry? Do you feel that faith and trust are the opposite of worry?

2. In the introduction, the authors discuss the Myers-Briggs personality questionnaire. Have you taken the Myers-Briggs? How would you rate your level of neuroticism, and how do you think that affects the other aspects of your Myers-Briggs results?

3. Will talks about being genuinely and justifiably worried as his son battles illness. Have you ever felt this way? How did it differ from your normal experiences of worry?

4. "Worriers need to stay with the threats they perceive long enough to realize they don't actually pose a risk" (page 34). Have you ever discovered that an object of your worry was actually harmless? How did you discover this, and how did it change your perspective on that thing afterward?

5. The authors discuss "floating worries," which are different from actionable concerns. What are your typical floating worries? How persistently do you worry about them?

6. Worry affects our bodies, our minds, and how we feel and make others around us feel. Often worriers will avoid situations that cause worry, but Will and Rob recommend facing worries head-on. What would this look like in your life? Is this a principle useful in other areas of life?

7. Worriers also worry about worrying. The authors are clear that compassion in your self-talk is key to avoiding a never-ending cycle of worry even as you work through the process of conquering your worry. How does it feel to try to bring compassion into your self-talk? What feelings and emotions do you end up confronting when you try to accept yourself without judgment?

8. The authors talk about the "magical thinking" of worrying—the idea that parents worrying about their bike-riding child can somehow, through worrying, prevent an accident. How have you found those kinds of magical thinking in your own life? Is there any validity to the idea that our thoughts can change reality?

9. How does your worry change the people around you? How have you found your worry affecting your family, friends, the people you love?

10. Will talks about riding roller coasters solely for how it represents his conquering worry. Do you resonate with his phrase "I feel afraid—yes! Bring it on"? What are activities you could do that would give you the opportunity to feel afraid and yet soldier on in spite of that fear?

11. The authors talk about superstitious actions such as creating tests for God (like Gideon's fleece) or using Bible verses as fortune-telling devices. Have you ever tried any of those techniques to alleviate your worry? Did they work? Why do you think they did or did not?

12. "The paradox of any search for certainty is that it invariably creates the opposite sentiment: doubt!" (page 111). Have you found this to be true? Why do you think that is? Is there certainty to be found in anything?

13. "Indeed, we follow a Savior whose journey led to the cross and crucifixion, so it would seem odd for us to wish for a stress-free life" (page 175). What does this mean for you? Are Christians able to live stress-free?

14. Present contemplation is one of the techniques the authors recommend as a spiritual practice for overcoming worry. Try this and then reflect on the experience. How did you feel during the contemplative practice? How could this practice help you in your journey toward healing?

15. After reading this book, do you feel prepared to commit to the hard work of healing from excessive worry? What steps do you think will be the easiest? The hardest?

Enhance Your Book Club

1. Share the answers from your exercises with the group. Talk about which ones you found easy and which were more difficult. Discuss your experiences: are you comfortable with overcoming worry, and where do you need the most help?

2. Exercise: Play a game where each person writes down an everyday activity on a note card. For example, "Drive the car to the mall and go shopping." Pass the cards to your left. On the card you receive write down one possible disaster that could take place. For example, "Crash the car" or "Get mugged" or "Nothing at the mall fits me." Pass the card to your left again and on the next card you receive write down a new disaster—make sure it's worse than the ones that came before it. When your card gets back around to you, read the worst-case scenarios on the cards and discuss how likely they are. Plan an activity that would challenge the anxieties of your group. Be smart, though: going on a roller coaster, riding the subway—good ideas. Jumping off of a roller coaster or licking a subway bathroom floor—bad ideas.

Author Questionnaire

How did you two find each other in order to write a book together?
Rob and I first met at the University of Cambridge, where Rob was reading medicine and I was reading theology and education. We had remained friends but reconnected professionally in 2006 at The Boat

Race, where we discussed our shared passion for Christian spirituality and mental health. We have been working and writing together as Mind and Soul (www.mindandsoul.info) ever since.

Worry is a difficult subject for churches. How can the church community as a whole encourage and empower worriers to be more open about their struggles without fear of pat answers or platitudes? How do you see churches actually contributing to the anxiety of their members?

We think it is essential that churches be more open to listening to human struggle across the board, not just in the area of worry. If church culture is closed and judgmental, people tend to keep up pretenses and a lot of dysfunction remains hidden just below the surface. If, however, churches are places where people feel safe to express their true hurts, fears, and anxieties, there is real hope for healing and restoration.

In the worst cases, churches can compound the anxieties of their members by making human emotions tantamount to sin. Stigma can be rife. The reality, however, is that Jesus was the most emotionally complete person ever to live, expressing the full range of feelings.

In your experience with people who worry, what is the most difficult part of overcoming worry?

In our opinion it is twofold. First, it is the "overestimation of threat" aspect. This leaves people convinced that their worries are more realistic than they really are. Second is the "intolerance of uncertainty" aspect, as this sends people on an eternal search for an assurance that can never be found. Once these two problems have been overcome (or at least defined and explained as uncertain and unsolvable with the usual problem-solving techniques), recovery comes much more easily.

How do the worries of the Western world compare with the worries in other parts of the world? Have you worked with anyone outside the American context?

Will: I have worked in Africa, where there are very real threats that we don't face in Europe or America, such as cholera or malaria. You may think that these threats would make African people more worried than us, or that we should worry less and be thankful for our lot. However, people are typically people and everyone in both the developing world and the Western world suffers from worry. People's themes may differ but their emotions are a universal human component!

When surfing in Australia as an Englishman I was amazed at how relaxed the Australians were about sharks. I was terrified! Having surfed with Australians in England I am amazed about how worried they are about the cold. I don't care! The key thing is that the worry is out of proportion to the threat and has an impact on how the person is living.

Are there philosophies and religions that have a better handle on worry?

We honestly think that Jesus's teaching in Matthew 6 is the best and most liberating teaching on worry in the history of the world. We just wish that Christian pastors and teachers were better at explaining it in the way that Jesus intended it! We have devoted part of the book to this.

We recommend some things that are nonreligious (such as techniques to get a good night's sleep), some things that most religions and philosophies share (like the ideas of contemplation and being mindful), and some things that are unique to Christianity (the role of prayer, a focus on a compassionate Jesus, and a hope of better things to come).

Christians seem especially prone to judging and guilt. Why do you think this is?

Well, that is a question we hoped you would ask, since it is the subject of our forthcoming book on the problem of guilt, which we hope will also be available through Simon & Schuster!

Will, tell us about the London bombings—how are they still affecting you, your family, your congregation?

The London bombings had a really big impact upon my life, and obviously that strongly affected my wife, Louie. I have moved out of central London now, but I know my old church still carries the emotion impact of that difficult time. Obviously, compared with 9/11 the London bombings were a relatively small event, but any trauma of that kind, particularly because it was caused deliberately, has a very powerful impact upon you and your community.

I travel on the tube (subway) every week and I still get nervous sometimes, especially if there is someone in my carriage with a lot of luggage. Even though I was not on one of the trains, these things live on in the imagination and can be powerful in triggering episodes of worry.

Are there any stories of worriers that you had to cut from the book? It's always nice to hear about people with worse problems than you.
We have aimed this book at people who struggle with worry but do not need professional help. It is based on cognitive therapy principles, but some people will need actual therapy from a trained cognitive behaviour therapist.

Rob: In my work, I have met people whose worry has caused them to lose weight and all their friends, or whose worries about future events such as the afterlife and sins they might have committed have left them severely affected by obsessive-compulsive disorder and also limited their ability to enjoy their faith.

Will, you've talked on your blog about "growing down" when it comes to relating to people with mental health issues. Is this a concept that is applicable in many areas of life?
If there is one virtue that Jesus demonstrates more than any other, it is humility. He was the Humble King. Society today is so consumed with getting ahead by judging and boxing others that humility has become countercultural.

The concept of growing down came from watching my kids. I saw how accepting and open they were toward people. I guess that if modern-day "growing up" means becoming judgmental and ambitious at someone else's expense, we need to think about growing the other way!